The Mirror of Salvation

The Mirror of Salvation

[Speculum Humanæ Salvationis]

An Edition of British Library Blockbook G. 11784

Translation & Commentary
by Albert C. Labriola & John W. Smeltz

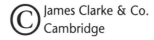

James Clarke & Co.
Cambridge

First published in the United Kingdom in 2002 by
James Clarke & Co Ltd
P.O. Box 60
Cambridge CB1 2NT
England
www.JamesClarke.co.uk
Publishing@JamesClarke.co.uk

ISBN 0 227 67969 5

British Library Cataloguing in Publication Data
A catalogue record is available from the British Library

Printed on acid-free paper in the United States of America.

Contents

Preface

We are grateful to the British Library for permission to reprint the 58 woodcuts, each composed of two illustrations and two captions, from *Speculum Humanae Salvationis* (shelfmark G.11784), a version of the blockbook probably produced in Holland in approximately 1470. This blockbook, whose title we translate concisely in English as *The Mirror of Salvation*, has 63 leaves, but the first five constitute the Preface in Latin verse, though without illustrations. The preface, which chiefly lists the topics of the 116 illustrations, serves in effect as a table of contents. We have replaced it with our own modern English version: a List of Woodcut Illustrations.

The blockbook whose woodcuts we have chosen to reprint is 19.5 centimeters (cm) wide and 26.8 cm long. Each woodcut is 19.5 cm wide and 10.7 cm long. The blockbook lacks a title page, pagination, and signatures. It was produced partly from wooden blocks and partly from moveable type, clearly an artifact that reflects the transition (in progress) from an older to a newer method of publication. In the older method of publication, blocks were carved with illustrations and text, then placed upright, presumably in a frame of sorts, and moistened with dye. In order to acquire the impression, paper was pressed downward onto this surface.

Each one of the 58 leaves that we have reprinted has a woodcut at the top, divided into two square compartments (left and right), each containing an illustration whose borders are circumscribed and decorated with architectural designs of columns and arches. These borders suggest that the illustrations were copied from the walls or windows of a cloister, chapel, church, convent, or monastery. The two illustrations in each woodcut do not constitute a horizontal diptych, for each is separate from the other.

Below each illustration and included inside the bottom of each compartment is a Latin sentence or phrase, a caption that recounts the event being depicted. And outside and below each compartment is a Latin text in verse, which comments on the illustration. The usual length of the Latin text is 25 lines. In this arrangement, each column, whether left or right, unfolds from top to bottom and is composed of the picture, the caption, and the commentary. All 58 illustrated leaves in the blockbook maintain this arrangement. Below our reprint of the woodcuts, we substitute our modern English prose translations for the commentaries or the 25 lines of Latin verse, all the while maintaining the double-column arrangement. Because these commentaries are often interrelated, they continue, at times, from the one to the next, and even on to another. In such cases the commentary is not end-stopped by punctuation such as a period, but open-ended with or without a comma while continuing into the commentary for the next illustration. Heading each column of our modern English translation of the Latin commentary is our translation of the caption for the illustration.

The biblical citations in the blockbook are to the Vulgate, the Latin translation by St. Jerome (ca. 345–420) of the original languages in which the Scriptures were written. We have therefore used the sixteenth century Douay Bible, which translates the Vulgate into English, for the titles of books of Scripture, the numbering of chapters and verses, and the spellings of personages and places. At times, of course, other versions of Scripture will differ from the Douay Bible in these details.

A. C. L. and J. W. S.
1 July 2001

INTRODUCTION

Introduction

Speculum Humanae Salvationis, concisely rendered in English as *The Mirror of Salvation*, is one of several medieval religious works that include "mirror" as part of the title. If one were to trace this term and its significance to a point of origin, 1 Corinthians 13.12 would be the *locus classicus*. In the figurative language of that text, Paul indicates that at present we see as in a mirror, which was made of polished metal in early antiquity, but in due course we will see face to face. By such figurative language, Paul contrasts our present perception of the godhead and of the hereafter with our later perception and experience, when we will directly encounter the deity and be ushered into eternity.

Another way of interpreting Paul's figurative language is to comprehend the temporal and spatial limitations of our present perception, while we anticipate our later view *sub specie aeternitatis*, when we will share in the expansive outlook of the godhead. For Paul, a mirror reflected, albeit imperfectly, its beholder (1 Corinthians 13.12). And in the human condition that same phenomenon distinguishes our recognition of the presence and manifestation of the Lord in Nature, in historical events, in other human beings, and even in ourselves. In the human condition and with our limited perception, we will not and cannot encounter the Lord face to face. While upholding faith in, and hope for, an apocalyptic future, religious literature with titles including "speculum" or "mirror" promotes our discernment of the Lord and of the workings of Providence in the past and present. Often the means for doing so was the "mirror" of history, most notably biblical history. Because Scripture both narrates and interprets history across a span of thousands of years, the dominant idea that emerges is one of salvation. In the saga of the Chosen People of Israel, the Christian view of history perceives a prophetic anticipation of the ministry of Jesus.

By interrelating the biblical history of the Hebrews with the ministry of Jesus, Christian exegetes or interpreters viewed many reflections, as in a mirror, of the history of salvation. Called biblical typology, this process aligns Old Testament types with New Testament antitypes. Types include personages, events, and even objects from Hebraic history that foreshadow and prefigure, but are fulfilled by, their counterparts or antitypes in the Christian era. If, as Christians contend, salvation ensues from the life, death, and Resurrection of Jesus, then such crucial events are foreshadowed and prefigured by the activities of Hebraic prophets, priests, patriarchs, and kings. These Hebraic precursors of Jesus delivered the Chosen People from captivity, enhanced their military might to overcome various adversaries, motivated their contrition after transgressions against the Lord, and reaffirmed their religious fidelity to him. Jesus reenacted all these activities but with transcendent implications and consequences. For he liberated his followers from enslavement to the power of evil, triumphed over Satan and the power of darkness, motivated the changeover from sinfulness to sanctification among his followers, and restored their loving relationship with the Lord.

The foregoing correlations, which center upon salvation, reflect a typological means of organizing and presenting biblical history. For instance, Hebraic types include Moses, the liberation of the Chosen People from Egypt, and the wooden rod or staff by which Moses performed signs and wonders that were approved and empowered by the Lord (Exodus 4–15). And the respective Christian antitypes are Jesus, his deliverance of captives during the harrowing of Hell, and his triumphal cross, not the cross of suffering, as an instrument of weaponry and retribution and an emblem of ultimate victory against his adversaries.

The biblical typology that we have recounted originated in the

Gospels, which employ it as a principle of organization and inter-pretation. The Gospels abound with (what we call) cross references to the Old Testament. When, for example, Jesus elaborates on the new law (Matthew 5–7), he does so by explicit reference to the old law as promulgated by Moses. Furthermore, in John 3.14–15, Jesus likens himself to the brazen serpent that Moses uplifted on a pole (Numbers 21.6–9) after the Israelites had been bitten by the so-called fiery serpents. Much as the afflicted Israelites by gazing on the brazen serpent were restored to health and their lives pro-longed, so also the faithful will attain to eternal life because Jesus has been lifted up on the cross. Furthermore, at the outset of Gos-pels of Matthew and Luke, the infancy narratives provide cross ref-erences to Old Testament passages that predicted the birth of the Messiah. And Paul's epistles, like the Gospels, emphasize biblical typology. In the Epistle to the Romans, for instance, Paul, while declaring that the Mosaic covenant must yield to the covenant of Jesus, uses biblical typology as a mirror in which to discern the workings of Providence.

Presumably the Gospels and Paul's epistles account for the typo-logical organization of the *The Mirror of Salvation*, though the more proximate influence may have been *The Bible of the Poor* or *Biblia Pauperum*. Both *The Mirror of Salvation* and *The Bible of the Poor* exist as manuscripts and as blockbooks. Manuscripts of *The Bible of the Poor* date back to the twelfth century, well before counter-parts of *The Mirror of Salvation* appear. And as a blockbook, *The Bible of the Poor* (ca. 1460) precedes *The Mirror of Salvation* by approximately ten years. It seems likely, therefore, that the earlier work registered some impact on the later one in various ways, not only in typological organization but also in the sequence of scenes from biblical history.

As a 40-leaf blockbook, the most typical form in which it appears, *The Bible of the Poor* has an iconographic triptych on each leaf. Beneath each triptych are a few quotations from Scripture and brief commentary. The central panel in the trifold arrangement features a scene from the New Testament, and the flanking panels depict

personages, events, and objects from the Old Testament. In each of
the 40 triptychs, the panels at the left and right portray the types
that prefigure and foreshadow, but are fulfilled by, the antitype in
the central panel. Furthermore, the temporal sequence of *The Bible
of the Poor* unfolds in the central panels. The 40 scenes from the
New Testament begin with the Annunciation and end with the
crowning of the righteous soul in the heavenly hereafter. Emphasized in the scenes from the New Testament are the birth, infancy,
childhood, and three-year public mininstry of Jesus, culminating in
his Passion, Crucifixion, and Resurrection.

Like its precursor, *The Mirror of Salvation* is organized along
similar typological lines and progresses according to its depiction of
scenes from the Christian era. The later blockbook is composed of
29 chapters, each of which includes four illustrations. The first two
chapters are exceptional in their depiction of only Old Testament
history. Beginning with the third chapter, however, the first of the
four illustrations is from the Christian era while the other three
are almost always from the Old Testament. This pattern continues
throughout the blockbook, with a single exception: The last chapter
has two (of four) illustrations from the New Testament. Accompanying each illustration in *The Mirror of Salvation* is commentary in
Latin verse, which highlights how and why the Old Testament prefigures and foreshadows, but is fulfilled by, the New Testament. In
some of its chapters, *The Mirror of Salvation* — unlike *The Bible of
the Poor*, which is wholly biblical in content — uses not only Old
Testament history but also the Apocrypha and even mythology to
identify types for the Christian antitypes. In such cases, non-
canonical Scriptural narratives and so-called heathen mythology
are accommodated to the typological framework, for the blockbook
shows that universal, not simply biblical, history has also been
imprinted providentially. Universal history, in sum, is fulfilled in
the Christian era, which illuminates retrospectively the panorama
of time that precedes it.

In this typological framework, chapters 3–7 of *The Mirror of
Salvation* focus on the Virgin Mary's role in the salvation of

humankind, and the remaining chapters, 8–29, dwell on Jesus as the savior. The progress of the blockbook, therefore, issues from the scenes of the Christian era, beginning with the life of Mary and proceeding thereafter to and through the life of Jesus: his birth, infancy, and childhood. Emphasizing his public ministry and the Passion, Crucifixion, and Resurrection, the blockbook proceeds to Doomsday and the Final Judgment, with Jesus overseeing the disposition of souls, whether to damnation or salvation, in the hereafter.

Concerning the interpretation of Scripture, the church fathers provided a legacy to later generations. But readers who lacked direct knowledge of Patristic exegesis could and did engage interpretively how and why the idea of salvation predominated in the pictures, captions, and commentaries of *The Mirror of Salvation*. As a self-contained and self-sufficient resource, *The Mirror of Salvation* did not require extraordinary erudition on the part of its readers. For it provides concise, simplified, and derivative commentaries from the church fathers, from numerous compendia for homilies and catechesis, from the proceedings of the various councils of the Church, and the like. The commentaries are unannotated, except for occasional biblical citations, because the aim of the blockbook, presumably, is to organize, synopsize, and to present cogently some traditional commentary on the idea of salvation and to do so in a manner that would both instruct and edify primarily the common folk.

The chief users of the *The Mirror of Salvation* were the clergy, for whom it was a veritable reference guide and resource for teaching the common folk and to whom it became available because of rapid and inexpensive reproduction as a blockbook. Through its commentaries, the blockbook articulates and implies, while enabling its readers to infer, multiple interpretations of its visual and verbal contents. Because, in such cases, the informing principle is the idea of salvation, all roads in effect lead to the same destination. In other words, the blockbook came into being not as a scholarly redaction of commentary on Scripture but as a means of educating the common folk in a manner commensurate with their level of understanding and their emotional involvement in expressing praise and gratitude to the Lord. These beliefs inform our approach to the blockbook, for we are not interested in identifying and annotating so-called sources and analogues of the commentaries in *The Mirror of Salvation*. Though laudable, such an effort is both tangential to our enterprise and conjectural at best because it is not possible to ascertain where the anonymous compilers of *The Mirror of Salvation* derived the commentaries. The unknown compilers were presumably clergymen, and almost surely monks, who in their commentaries synopsized longstanding traditional views on Scripture.

In line with what we affirm above, we do what has never before been done in a reprint of the woodcuts. That is, we identify the details of the illustrations and interpret their significance by referring to the biblical texts, the Apocrypha, and mythological legends cited in the commentaries by the anonymous compilers. Our interpretations manifest a process of discernment that accords with the predominant idea of salvation promulgated in the very title of the blockbook. To the degree that such is possible and in order to bridge the gap of history, we strive to enact the process whereby a medieval reader, guided by the pictures, captions, and commentaries in the blockbook, might interpret the roles of Mary and then of Jesus in the salvation of humankind.

From the preceding account, it should be evident that our goals are simple and straightforward and that they accord with our beliefs about the origin and use of the blockbook. We aim to present the illustrations, captions, and commentary of *The Mirror of Salvation* in an immediately accessible and understandable form and to the widest possible present-day audience. We aim, as well, to interpret the visual and verbal contents of *The Mirror of Salvation* in a manner consonant with the idea of salvation and in a way that exemplifies how a user of the blockbook would have found it a useful resource for teaching the common folk. We have, therefore, produced the first and only modern English translation of *The Mirror of Salvation* and the one and only systematic interpretation of its

contents. We hope, therefore, that our work will encourage readers
in the following ways:

1. to renew interest in how Scripture was adapted for the
instruction of the common folk;

2. to promote comparative study between *The Mirror of Salvation* and *The Bible of the Poor*, with which it overlaps at
times in illustrating and commenting on certain biblical events
and personages;

3. to encourage analysis of how *The Mirror of Salvation*
interacts with medieval religious literature, most notably
cycle-dramas, narrative poetry, legends involving scriptural
personages, and the Apocrypha;

4. to highlight how the illustrations in *The Mirror of Salvation*
may be related to late medieval religious art and architecture,
such as Gothic cathedrals and the biblical scenes in their
windows and sculptures;

5. to suggest how the blockbook provides a context for understanding Renaissance religious art that focuses on the history
of salvation, including Michelangelo's frescoes in the Sistine
Chapel, which visualize a panorama of biblical episodes and
personages;

6. to perceive *The Mirror of Salvation* as manifesting (what
we will call) the genre "Mirror," another example of which is
Vincent of Beauvais's *Speculum Universale*, composed, in turn,
of the *Speculum Naturale*, *Speculum Doctrinale*, and *Speculum Historiale*;

7. to demonstrate how Christian exegetes accommodated
mythological legends, many of which are illustrated in *The
Mirror of Salvation*, to an understanding of biblical history and
the promise of salvation;

8. to motivate readers to investigate manuscript versions,
early printed copies, and more recent editions of *The Mirror of
Salvation*, and to consult scholarship concerning this blockbook.

Many other purposes may be served by the ready and easy access to *The Mirror of Salvation* that we have provided, not all of which can be stated or even anticipated. For when such a work, as we have chosen to present it, reaches an enlarged reading audience, the implications are far-reaching and wide — professionally and personally.

THE BLOCKBOOK

List of the Woodcut Illustrations

Chapter 18

Chapter 19

Chapter 20

Chapter 21

Chapter 22

Chapter 23

Plates and Text (in translation)

Chapter 1

Figure 1. **Fall of Lucifer**

Figure 2. **God created man in his own image and likeness**

Here begins the Mirror of our Salvation, the story of the fall, the redemption, and an explanation of why God created man. In this Mirror we shall learn how a trick of the devil damned us and how the mercy of God will save us. The drama begins when Lucifer rose up against his creator, the eternal God, and in the blink of an eye is hurled from the heights of heaven to the depths of hell. To restore the loss of Lucifer and his companions, God decides to create the human race, and on this account the devil, envious of man, plots against him, and plans to tempt him to disobey the commandments of God. He therefore disguises himself as a serpent that walks upright and has the face of a maiden. The great deceiver, a master of a thousand wiles, puts on this disguise to deceive Eve, judging her to be less cautious than prudent Adam. Next, he approaches the woman when she is alone and is easier to convince without her companion. He then finally deceives our mother, Eve, bringing cruel death into this world. It must be remembered that man was created in a field near Damascus and later moved to Paradise by the Lord.

Here in the garden the Lord creates woman from the side of Adam while he sleeps. He thus honors her to a certain degree above her husband since she is created not from clay but from the bone and the flesh of the noble Adam. She is not made from a foot lest she be looked down upon, nor does she spring from his head lest she rule over him, but rather she is fashioned from his side and given to man to be his companion and helpmate. If she had humbly persevered in honor, never would she have endured any hostility from man. Because she believed the devil and not her husband, she merits punishment and humiliation. Later, Adam reluctantly consents to eat the fruit with his beloved whom he does not wish to sadden. Solomon once adored an idol, because of his love for a woman, whom he did not think to be a goddess. Likewise, Adam eats the fruit with Eve because of his love for her, without believing that he would be like God. Eve's sin is greater than that of her husband since she had wished to be like God, and over and above this desire she persuaded Adam to transgress God's commandment.

Chapter 1

Figure 3. *You will eat of all the trees of Paradise*

Figure 4. *You will never die, but you will be like the Lord and know good and evil*

Although it is not found in the text of the Bible, it is certain that Eve had adulated Adam with flattering words. Be attentive, therefore, to the ability of a woman to deceive, and beware of her flattery lest you are beguiled. Behold Adam, the handiwork of God; look upon Samson the bravest; behold David, a man after the heart of God; and look upon Solomon the wisest. If these great men were deceived by the skill of a woman, how are we to be safe? Satan does not dare to tempt Adam, but Eve, bolder than Satan, presumes to deceive her husband. So Satan deceives the woman, who dooms, in turn, Adam and all his posterity. If man had kept the commandments of God, he would never taste punishment or death, nor endure weakness, weariness, sickness, and care, and would be born without weeping, wailing, and labor. He never would know grief and anxiety nor endure shame and distress. He would never become deaf, lose teeth, become blind, or grow lame. He never would drown in a river or a well,

nor be harmed by fire or the heat of the sun. Neither beast nor bird would ever attack him, and neither the air nor the breeze would infect him. Never would men have argued, but would have respected each other as brothers. Every creature would have been subject to him, and he would have lived in joy forever without care. When it pleased God, he would have taken man, body and spirit, to heaven. No one dares to investigate why God created man who he knew would fall, why he created the angels whose fall he certainly foresaw, why he allowed the heart of King Pharao to harden and the heart of penitent Mary Magdalen to soften, why he forgave Peter for his three denials but allowed Judas to despair because of his sin, why he granted the grace of conversion to the one thief but did not trouble himself to grant a similar grace to his companion, and why He forgives one sin and not another. No one, no matter how wise he may be, may presume to investigate the works of God, nor the inscrutable nature of man. Paul briefly addresses the question, "God rejects whom He wills, but is merciful to whom He wishes" (Romans 9.18).

Chapter 2

*Figure 5. **Eve deceives Adam to eat with her***

*Figure 6. **An Angel with a flaming sword cast Adam and Eve from the garden***

In the first chapter we have seen how God honored man; let us now consider how man judges himself to be of little value. When Adam was in God's favor, he did not value his own gifts. Thus, he is expelled from the earthly paradise because he places himself in opposition to God, his creator, and is thereby cast from the garden of delight to this vale of misfortune. Not a little uncertain about his gifts, Adam chooses pain and sorrow. He leaves the earthly paradise, a joyous and delightful place, and enters a world full of adversity and sorrow, deception and deceit, a world full of hollow promises. The world holds out the promise of a long life, but when death comes, man has neither the strength nor the power to prolong his life for an instant. The world promises him long lasting health, but introduces the body and soul to perpetual infirmity. The world promises him riches and honor, but gives him decay and stench. However, sometimes the world favors man, but prosperity is fleeting and vain, and man is unable to prolong life or defend against the power of death. In this extreme need the world does not offer man any help, but with much pretense gives the body the most inexpensive shroud. The world appears to be like an elder tree whose flower is beautiful but whose fruit is bitter just as worldly pleasures appear to be delightful but their fruit is eternal damnation. The world gives a signal, just as Judas gave a signal to Christ's enemies. The sign that the world gives to the demon is to bestow riches and honors on an individual and then torment him for all eternity; the sign Judas gave to the enemies of Christ is a kiss: "Whomever I shall kiss, that is he, seize him" (Matthew 26.48). However, riches do not always lead to damnation, but may even help many on the way to salvation; Daniel said to King Nabuchodonosor, "Redeem your sins with alms" (Daniel 4.24). God does not abandon the powerful if riches are used for temporal good. Tobias taught his son, "If you have much, give abundantly, if you have little, take care to give a little willingly" (Tobias 4.9). Riches do not condemn a person, love of riches does; food does not defile a man, excessive use does. Fine attire does not cause one to sin if the heart has been given to God, for anyone clothed according to his state is without sin. It is not fitting for a king to be clothed in sackcloth, nor a peasant adorned in fine silk. Therefore, let everyone use his possessions according to his state and guard most diligently lest he go to excess.

Chapter 2

*Figure 7. **Here Adam with sweat on his brow delves the earth***

*Figure 8. **The ark of Noe***

In every endeavor follow moderation and avoid excess assiduously, for the world betrays us by ministering to our concupiscence. We must overcome an unruly appetite with constraint and a sense of duty. We would not undergo these assaults by the world if we had remained in Paradise free from hardships, but now we scarcely endure an hour without some difficulty. Now known enemies lie in wait for us, close friends try to cheat us, and even the smallest gnats and flies annoy us. Deservedly, the elements and the creatures of the earth assail us because Adam raised himself up against God. The earth torments us with thorn and thistle, and the beasts lacerate us with horn and teeth. The sea engulfs us in floods and tempests, and pirates fall upon us with violent plundering and pillaging. Even the air carries pestilences to infect us, and the birds wound us with bill and talon. Fire reduces the flesh and bones to ashes, and the smoke of the fire spreads gloom over our eyes. There are no enemies in Paradise, but one rarely finds true friends here. As long as we possess riches and status,

we have many friends and patrons, but when help is needed scarcely will one assist. True friends are manifested in time of need, for whoever is present at a time of adversity, tends our wounds, or exposes himself to dangers for us exhibits an abundance of charity. Our most clement Savior has even greater charity, for he exposed himself to danger for his enemies, us. We are the enemies of God condemned to this prison, but through his mercy we are set free. There is no escape from this prison; however, the father of mercy and consolation looks upon our fall mercifully and decrees to save us. Concerning this matter he gives us a sign, the olive branch the dove brought back to show those in the ark the mercy of God. The olive branch is not only a sign for those in the ark, but also a foreshadowing of our salvation. God has foretold our salvation in many figures and types that become evident from a diligent study of Divine Scripture. O good Jesus, teach us to understand the Sacred Scriptures and have the ability to perceive your charity in them.

Chapter 3

Figure 9. **Here the birth of Mary is announced**

Figure 10. **King Astyages has an extraordinary dream**

Seeing that we now desire to know the story of our salvation, let us start at the beginning, the annunciation of the birth of Mary. Before considering the blessed incarnation of Christ, it is necessary to take into account the lineage of his mother. A subject introduced by a parable or story is more easily understood, and this is the way we shall begin. A certain man went down from Jerusalem to Jericho (Luke 10.29–36). As he was passing through the desert, he came unexpectedly upon thieves who beat him, robbed him, and then fled, having left him for dead. A priest and a Levite came by. Both did not care for his injuries but continued on their journey. Finally, a Samaritan passed by, and moved by compassion, he dressed the poor man's wounds. Had he not passed by, the injured man would never have been treated. This parable applies to every man who was cast out of Paradise and placed in this desert. Because they squandered the goods and graces God gave them, they are smitten by the wound of mortality. For a long time man lies half dead, alive in body, but dead in spirit. Neither priest nor Levite is able to heal him, and neither circumcision nor money could guide him back to his true home. Finally a certain Samaritan came by,

and mercifully treated the wounded man. The Samaritan is Jesus Christ, our protector; if our protector had not come into this world, we would never gain eternal life. Let us praise and bless Our Lord Jesus Christ who came to heal half-dead humanity! When the Son of God prepared to come into this world, he ordained that he would be born of virgin. He sent an angel to announce her conception, name, and sanctification in the womb. She is indeed the Most Blessed Virgin Mary through whom a gentle cure came for the wounded, a remedy shown in advance in many figures and events made known by the prophets. King Astyages had a dream of a most beautiful vine that grew out of his daughter; the vine had leaves and branches bearing fruit and spread out over his entire kingdom. The following interpretation was reported to him: that a great king was about to be born to his daughter. Some time after the dream the daughter gave birth to King Cyrus who later freed the children of Israel from the Babylonian Captivity. This is the literal meaning of the dream, but there is also a mystical interpretation of the same event.

Chapter 3

ortus conclusus fons signatus   balaam prudatut ortu marie stella

Figure 11. **An enclosed garden, a sealed fountain**

Figure 12. **Balaam through a star prophesied the birth of Mary**

To Astyages it is shown that his daughter would give birth to Cyrus the king; to Joachim it is announced that his daughter would bear Christ the King. Cyrus liberated the Jews from the Babylonian Captivity, and Christ the King frees us from the bondage of Satan. Therefore, the daughter of Astyages prefigures Mary, who shows the world a morally correct and faithful life. May you be blessed, O daughter of the sovereign king, a dazzling white flower surpassing the lily! May the annunciation of your conception be blessed because it is the beginning of our release from captivity! Blessed be God the Father who predestined you for us! Blessed be God the Son who adopts you for a mother! Blessed be God the Holy Spirit who sanctifies you before your birth! Blessed be both your parents who brought you into the world! Most assuredly, Solomon had foretold the coming of this daughter who was hallowed before birth; he called her an enclosed garden and a fountain sealed in the Canticle of Canticles (4.12). While her mother Anna bore her, the Holy Spirit pours grace into her soul and signs her with the seal of the Holy Trinity so that no sin ever defiles her. Truly, Mary, you are the garden of happiness and the unfailing fountain for the thirsting souls. The Holy Spirit makes you known to us when he prophesied your birth through the mouth of Balaam.

Balaam promised that a star prefiguring Mary would arise from the tribe of Jacob and would be the future dwelling place of God. Also Balaam cursed the people of Israel, but the Holy Spirit shows, figuratively, how the curse of Eve is changed to a blessing. A maiden whose birth is prefigured by a star brings about this transformation. This star of the sea is indeed the most Blessed Mary, the guide and the rescuer of those tossed on the deep. Without this star we are unable to navigate the tempestuous seas of this world and arrive safely at the port of our heavenly home. God foretold the birth of Mary by a star to map out for us our return home, and we thank Him for this guide for our perilous journey. O sinners, no matter how much you have sinned, do not despair! Look to this star with the eyes of your heart and in doubt, danger, and need let it be your guide as Theophilus looked upon it to lead him from his enemy to a safe port. O good Jesus, give us this star to contemplate so we may merit to escape every peril.

Chapter 4

uatiuitas glose virgis mane   egrdiemr uga te inatce pelle

Figure 13. **The nativity of the glorious Virgin Mary**

Figure 14. **A branch will spring from the root of Jesse**

In the previous chapter, we have heard the story of the annunciation of the Blessed Virgin, and now let us consider her birth and lineage. The ancestry of Mary descends from the father of David [i.e., Jesse], about whom Isaias, inspired by the Holy Spirit, prophesied, "There shall come forth a rod out of the root of Jesse and a flower shall bloom from this root, and upon this flower the sevenfold grace of the Holy Spirit shall rest" (Isaias 11.1–2). This rod signifies Mary who is made fruitful by a heavenly dew and produces for us Christ, the most beautiful flower. In this flower are found seven efficacious remedies, which beget the Seven Gifts of the Holy Spirit. The seven remedies for the sickness of the soul are touch, perfume, fruit, color, leaf, juice, and taste, all contraries to the seven deadly sins. By touching this flower we reduce the tumor of pride and become humble to receive the gift of fear and a greater self-knowledge. When we meditate how Lucifer is punished for the arrogance of pride, we become humble and begin to fear God. If God is unwilling to endure pride in Lucifer's angels, much less does he wish to tolerate it in us. The angels had a special grace by which they were glorified, but what does lowly man have, and how shall he be glorified? By the perfume of this flower the hardness of the envious heart is softened

begetting the gift of piety to extend compassion to the afflicted. An envious sinner is not touched by suffering, but a pious person is moved to pity and mercy by every hardship. This perfume is the example our Savior places before us. Because he is merciful and compassionate toward the afflicted, we, following his lesson, lament with those who weep and agonize in spirit with those who suffer in body. The fruit of the flower removes the madness of anger and teaches us the gift of science to live in harmony with our neighbors. The wrathful person has no mental circumspection and is unable to engage in good and decent conversation, but the gift of science teaches us to live well in this depraved society. Therefore, whosoever wishes to imitate the fruit of this flower, the works of Christ, must learn to live in harmony with others. By the color of this flower the paralysis of wrath is weakened and we are strengthened by the gift of fortitude to persevere. He who understands that the color of this flower represents Christ crucified neither dreads work nor suffers any punishment. If indeed an elephant fights at the sight of the blood of grapes (1 Machabees 6.34), how much more are we strengthened to work by the sight of the blood of Christ. Therefore, we devoutly gaze upon the rose color of this flower and labor cheerfully to persevere all our days. By the leaves of this flower we put to flight the dropsy of avarice and curb the desire for money by the gift of counsel.

Chapter 4

Figure 15. *The closed door signifies the blessed Virgin Mary*

Figure 16. *The Temple of Solomon signifies the Blessed Mary*

The leaves of this flower are the words, works, and doctrine of Christ, all counseling us to despise the temporal and seek the eternal. Whoever endeavors diligently to study and retain this doctrine has the spirit of counsel within him and despises temporal possessions except for what is needed to help the indigent. By the juice of this flower the excess of gluttony is reduced, and through the gift of understanding we acquire knowledge. The green juice of the flower helps us to see more clearly, and the gift of understanding purifies the eye of the heart. Further, the gift of understanding teaches us to know the divine through the material. When we see the sun so bright or a flower so beautiful, we shall understand the sun's brilliance and the flower's beauty are from the creator. By the taste of this flower the sweetness of luxury turns sour and the soul delights in the gift of wisdom, the relishing of knowledge. After we have tasted the sweetness of the Holy Spirit, all pleasures of the flesh are bitter. Just as honey dulls the natural taste of food, so too relishing the Holy Spirit puts an end to all carnal pleasures. O how great is your sweetness, O Lord, hidden from those who fear you! Therefore, it is now evident that Mary is born in the line of Jesse, but how the flower blossomed is revealed in the figure of the closed door. Ezechiel in a vision beheld the closed door,

which would never be opened for all eternity (Ezechiel 44.1–3). Only the Lord could pass through the closed door, a figure for Christ's miraculous birth. Let him who is able understand! Christ was not born in the same way we are born. It would not be a wondrous event to open a door and pass through, but it is exceedingly miraculous to pass through a closed door. Also, Solomon built a temple dedicated to the Lord that mystically prefigured the birth of the Blessed Mary. The temple had three pinnacles to signify Mary's triple golden celestial crown: the first crown signifies virginity, for this is the way she is known; the second is the crown of martyrs, for she is a martyr in spirit; and the third is the crown of preachers and teachers because she is the master of the evangelists and the apostles. The exterior of the temple was constructed of dazzling white marble and the interior was decorated with the most elegant gold. Mary radiates the dazzling splendor of the purest chastity and inwardly possesses the gold of the most precious charity. O how radiantly beautiful is the chaste generation! O how beautiful is Mary resplendent with charity! There was a ladder in the temple used to climb upward; in Mary is a divinity, a grace opening for us an ascent to heaven. O good Jesus grant through the merits of your most holy mother the ability to ascend to the glory of God the Father.

Chapter 5

Figure 17. **In the temple Mary is presented to the Lord**

Figure 18. **The golden table in the sand is presented in the temple of the sun**

In the preceding chapter we have heard the story of the birth of the Blessed Virgin; let us now consider how she is presented to the Lord in the temple. When she was three years old, her parents presented her to the Chief Priest of the temple to study and to serve God. This presentation is prefigured by the story of the fishermen who cast their net into the sea and by a wondrous stroke of good fortune pulled out of the sea a precious and exceedingly beautiful table made of pure gold and whose beauty was evident to all who saw it. On the shore opposite the sea where the table was found, the people of the community built a temple and dedicated it to the sun. They then carried the golden table to the temple and presented it to the sun as though they were offering it to a god. Throughout the world the table is called, "The Table of the Sun in Sabulo." The definition of the word "sabulum" is sandy ground since the temple of the sun was built in a sandy place. Mary is aptly prefigured by this table, for she is presented to the true sun, the supreme God. The table of the sun is offered in the temple of the material sun, but Mary is presented in the temple of the eternal sun. Many angels and men came to see the birth of Mary, just as men and nobles journeyed to see the table. The table of the sun is made of the finest material,

just as Mary is most pure in mind and body. This table prefigures the purity of Mary because through her a heavenly food is given to us. She assuredly gave birth to Jesus Christ, the Son of God, who revives us with his own body and blood. Blessed be Mary, this most precious table, and the banquet given to us so salutary and beneficial! Blessed be her parents who offer her to the Lord for our salvation! We are unable to find anyone in the Old Testament who offers his or her own daughter to the Lord unless we consider Jephte (Judges 11.31–39), who sacrifices his daughter to the Lord. Jephte did not offer his daughter according to the law, but Joachim and Anna dedicate their young child to the Lord correctly and completely. They do not slay or sacrifice her but give her to the Lord alive to serve Him alone. Jephte's vow is censured by the holy doctors, but Mary's vow is praised by God and the angels. Jephte's daughter weeps because she would not have any children; but Mary at a young age promises to remain a virgin, and she also grieves that she would be childless, lamenting that the Christ would not be born of her. Mary weeps because she judges herself to be the most wretched, yet she found great joy in her vow. Jephte's daughter was offered in thanksgiving after a victory, but Mary is offered as a symbol of a victory before it took place.

Chapter 5

Figure 19. **Jephte sacrifices his daughter to the Lord**

Figure 20. **From atop the hanging garden, the Queen of Persia sees her homeland**

Jephte's daughter is sacrificed for a victory over temporal forces, but Mary is victorious over the eternal enemy. Because Jephte heedlessly offered his daughter to the Lord, she is unable to serve him afterward; but after her presentation Mary serves the Lord forever. How Mary serves God, and how she embraces her new life is prefigured by a garden sometimes called the hanging garden. The King of Persia planted a garden atop a tower from which it was possible for his wife to see her homeland from afar; this structure signifies the contemplative life of Mary who longed to look to her heavenly homeland from afar. She is ever attentive to devotion and prayer, never acquiring idle habits or worldly ways. She gives herself devoutly to contemplative prayer and applies herself diligently to work and study. She chants the psalms and hymns jubilantly, often weeping sweetly at prayer and devotion, imploring the Lord for our salvation without ceasing, and reading the Scriptures frequently about the coming of Christ. Whatever she finds in the Scriptures concerning the incarnation of God, she reads and rereads, kissing and treasuring the text. When other virgins return home to their families, she remains in the Lord's temple to study and read. Whatever needs to be washed in the temple, she washes, and what needs to be ceremonially purified, she purifies. Never does she become drowsy, and never does she sleep unless compelled by necessity. Even though the body sleeps, the interior of her soul is always awake just as Solomon described, "I sleep, but my heart is vigilant" (Canticle of Canticles 5.2). She lives prudently, humbly, and devoutly, and her life is an example for all who know her. Her speech is exceedingly discreet, moderate, always agreeable, pleasant, and never ill tempered. She never looks down upon the poor or the lame, and everyone greets her politely and she responds pleasantly. Over and above this characterization she is humble, compassionate, devout, and totally given to God and ever attentive to His will. She thoroughly understands the Books of the Prophets and Sacred Scripture insofar as the Holy Spirit, the best teacher, instructs her. Never does she cast her eyes upon a man, nor fix her glance upon one's countenance. Never does she carry her head erect, but her eyes are ever fixed on the ground, and her heart is always lifted heavenward. Whatever honor or praise is able to be said, written, or sung about her, that praise may be used in preaching about the Most Blessed Virgin. O good Jesus give us the ability to praise her now so that we may merit to dwell with you and her eternally!

Chapter 6

Figure 21. **Here the Virgin Mary marries Joseph**

Figure 22. **Here Sara marries young Tobias**

In the previous chapter we have learned how Mary was presented in the temple; now let us consider why and how she marries Joseph. There are eight reasons why God wants His mother to marry. The first reason is that it may not be thought she became pregnant as a result of fornication and therefore may be judged a sinner in a court of justice. Secondly, a maiden would benefit from the aid and support of a man, and wherever she may travel, she would not be considered a vagrant. Thirdly, that Satan not become aware of the Incarnation of the Son and not speculate that a maiden conceived without the help of a man. Fourthly, so Mary shall have a witness to her chastity since her husband will be believed more than anyone else. Fifthly, that a genealogical line be established through the husband, for it is a custom in Scripture to construct a family tree by using the husband's ancestors. Sixthly, that the marriage be valid and no one censure or reject it. Seventhly, that Mary may teach that it is lawful to pursue virginity in marriage if both husband and wife agree. Finally, the eighth reason — that those who are wedded should not despair by thinking that only virgins are among the elect. The Lord approves every state if one does his or her duty, and so his mother is a maiden, a wife, and finally a widow. These three states are indeed holy,

but each differs greatly from the other. Matrimony is judged to be holy and good if time, manner, and intent are duly adhered to, but the chastity of widowhood is better than wedlock, and virginal purity excels both and is the best state. To the married state is due spiritual fruit to the measure of thirtyfold, to the widows sixtyfold, and to virgins a hundredfold. Brass is said to be a precious metal, but silver is more precious, and gold is the most precious. Early in the morning the rising daystar appears to be bright; however, the moon is brighter, and the sun is the brightest. The joy and pleasure of this world seem to be delightful, and the pleasures of Paradise were more delightful, but the joys of heaven are the most delightful. Although virginity supersedes other states, it is worthless unless holiness of the soul is preserved. Those who are virgins according to the flesh but not according to the spirit will not receive the virgin's crown in heaven. Whoever shall remain a virgin in heart and spirit, though violently raped, will not lose the golden crown but rather will receive a double reward. Those persons will have a crown for virginity of spirit over and above the special reward for the brutality they suffered. A crown lost because of weakness may be re-stored in this life by contrition, but whoever is willfully corrupted in the flesh will be un-able to recover this crown by any amount of contrition.

Chapter 6

Figure 23. **The tower called Baris signifies Mary**

Figure 24. **A thousand shields hang from the tower of David**

Although Mary is joined to a man in wedlock, it is held that she remains a virgin in body and spirit for all eternity, and is able to say with Sara, daughter of Raguel, "I have kept my soul clean from all lust" (Tobias 3.16). Sara was married to seven men, yet she remained a virgin undefiled; how much more is it possible for Mary, having only one husband, to remain an immaculate virgin for all eternity. If Asmodeus protected Sara from seven husbands, should not the true God protect His mother from one man. Every time Joseph looks upon the mother of the Lord, he sees a divine splendor emanating from her and therefore never dares to look upon her face except by chance. Tobias and Sara were chaste for three nights, but Mary and Joseph remain virgins all their lives. Joseph, a virgin, and a descendant of David is joined to Mary by the will of God to be her protector and to shield her from suspicion. Also, Mary has our sovereign God for a safeguard to defend her from every assault of the enemy. Therefore, she has a heavenly protector and an earthly one too. Wherefore, this virgin is so holy and unique and

she is likened to a tower called Baris that could be defended from a vast multitude by only two sentries. So strong and invincible is Mary whose extraordinary defender is God that no assault of any enemy ever harmed her. On this account her life is compared to the tower of David protected by 1,000 shields. These shields represent all the virtues and all the good works used to defend the Virgin Mary. So greatly is she fortified and strengthened that she overcame every temptation and conquered every sin. She not only repels temptation and sin from herself but also from others to whom she then infuses the rays of her grace. Although the Virgin is exceedingly beautiful, never does anyone desire her, for a divine power emanates from her extinguishing the illicit concupiscence of those beholding her. Just as serpents flee the odor of the cypress tree, so also Mary puts to flight evil concupiscence by her grace. Just as serpents cannot dwell in a garden abounding with flowers, so too no evil concupiscence can come close to Mary. O good Jesus, remove all evil desires from us and fill our hearts with the gift of your clemency!

Chapter 7

Figure 25. **The annunciation by the angel to the Virgin Mary**

Figure 26. **The Lord in the burning bush appears to Moses**

Banderoles: Hail full of grace, the Lord is with you. Behold the handmaiden of the Lord, may it be done unto me according to your word.

In the last chapter we learned about the marriage of Mary; let us now consider her annunciation. After Mary had been married to Joseph in Jerusalem, she returns to her parents' home in Nazareth. In the meantime Joseph directs all his attention to the needs of their marriage, but unknown to him Mary had conceived by the Holy Spirit. Do not suspect that the angel found her in an unlocked chamber, for God is her only interest and she despises godless creatures. She does not wander about meddling as Dina did (Genesis 34.1–2), nor does she behave like Thamar, who dallies with men intimately (Genesis 38.13–18). Rather, Mary is like Sara, daughter of Raquel (Tobias 3.16), who never desires a man, and like solitary Judith devotes herself to prayer and fasting (Judith 8.4–6). Therefore, when Joseph finds her pregnant, he, fearing and trembling, is indeed confounded and resolves within his heart: "It is impossible this woman has conceived a child by fornication, considering how she has lived, so holy, chaste, and temperate. She is neither a glutton, drinker, or charmer, nor a chorine, dancer, or jester. She has always avoided public places, fled them as much as possible, and has always lived a solitary and contemplative life. She has rejected every comfort and joy and has delighted only in the divine and the heavenly. From childhood she had dwelt in the temple of the Lord and has had no dealings with men. Now after she returned home to her parents,

she prayed constantly in a closed chamber. Joseph speculates, "How is it possible for her to sin since she never gave anyone an occasion to sin? Perhaps the prophecy of Isaias is now fulfilled in her, 'Behold a Virgin shall conceive and bear a child' (Isaias 7.14). Perhaps this young maiden is of the seed of Jacob whom the Holy Spirit foretold through the mouth of Balaam by the sign of a star (Numbers 24.17). Balaam prophesied that the Holy Spirit wished to dwell in this maiden so that the Son of God would be born of a Virgin. Perhaps also this virgin may be the flowering rod prophesied to spring from the root of Jesse. Perhaps this is the virgin of whom Christ is to be born since it was prophesied he would be born of the seed of David, son of Jesse. Therefore, she may be judged to be a most holy virgin, and for that reason she is to be the mother of Christ. Since I am not worthy to dwell with such a virgin, I must not on that account fulfill our marriage, but must now secretly and cautiously dissolve the bond lest someone becomes suspicious." Joseph considers himself unworthy and fears to dwell with Mary; likewise, John fears to baptize Christ (Matthew 3.14); the centurion begs Christ not to enter his home (Matthew 8.8); Peter beseeches Christ to depart from his boat (Luke 5.8); the woman of the Sunamites fears to dwell with Eliseus (4 Kings 4.8–10). So Joseph now fears to dwell with Mary, the Mother of God.

Chapter 7

Figure 27. *Gedeon's fleece is soaked while the earth remains dry*

Figure 28. *Rebecca gives a drink to the servant of Abraham*

While Joseph is in this state of anxiety about Mary, an angel of the Lord is sent to him to put his mind to rest. The angel tells him not to leave Mary since she has conceived by the Holy Spirit, not by man. The conception so wondrous and great was prefigured when Moses beheld the burning bush (Exodus 3.2–14) that continued to burn but did not lose its verdure. Mary conceives a son but does not lose her virginity. The Lord inhabited the burning bush and the same God dwells in Mary. God descended into the burning bush for the liberation of the Jews, and the Lord inhabited Mary for our redemption. The Lord descended into the bush to lead the Jews out of Egypt, and he took up his abode in Mary to free us from Hell. When God wills to become man, he chooses Mary from all the women of the world. This event is prefigured by Gedeon's fleece, which became moist with heavenly dew, but only the fleece receives the dew while the entire surrounding area remains dry (Judges 6.36–40); likewise, Mary alone is filled with the divine dew, and no one else in the entire world is found worthy. Many daughters have gathered together riches (Proverbs 31.29), but Mary surpasses them all. Gedeon prayed that God would give him a sign in the fleece,

if the children of Israel would be free from their enemies. The moistening of the fleece is a sign of liberation, just as the conception is a sign of our redemption. The fleece of Gedeon is the Blessed Virgin Mary; and from this fleece is made a garment, Jesus Christ, true wisdom, who clothes himself in our humanity to invest us in the garment of everlasting joy. Gedeon's fleece receives the dew without any injury to the wool, and Mary conceives a son without any corruption to the flesh. Gedeon squeezes the dew out of the fleece and fills his tunic with it; Mary brings forth a son who fills the whole world with the dew of his grace. The conception of Mary occurs at the annunciation of the angel Gabriel, an event prefigured by Eliazar, a servant of Abraham, who is sent to seek a maiden for his master's son, Isaac, to wed. (Genesis 24.1–51). Rebecca gives the messenger a drink of water, and so the servant chooses her to be the spouse of Isaac. Likewise, the Heavenly Father sends his messenger, Gabriel, into the world to seek the Virgin to be the mother of his Son. Gabriel finds Mary to be the most suitable maiden, and she gives him a drink, her consent to his message. Rebecca gave a drink of water to the messenger and his camel, but Mary pledges the fount of life to the angels and to man. O good Jesus may we so venerate your incarnation that we may merit to have our thirst satisfied with a cup of water from the fount of life.

Chapter 8

Figure 29. **The Nativity of our Lord Jesus Christ**

Figure 30. **In a dream Pharao's cup bearer sees a vine in a dream**

In the last chapter we heard the story of Christ's conception; now let us consider his birth. The angels were not alone in their desire to witness his birth, but the holy and ancient fathers also desired, awaited, and prophesied his blessed nativity. "Send forth, O Lord, the lamb, the ruler of the earth" (Isaias 16.1). "Send forth your light and truth, eternal God" (Psalms 42.3). "Make your face shine upon us, and we shall be saved" (Psalms 30.17). Make your Son known whom we are expecting and seeking, "O that you would rend the heavens and come down" (Isaias 64.1). To liberate us from the bondage of the devil, "Lord bow down the heavens and descend" (Psalms 143.5). Extend your right hand to free us and "remember your mercies that are from the beginning of the world" (Psalms 24.6). Come and "deliver us from the power of darkness" (Colossians 1.13). Come O Lord, so your prophets are trusted and true, your promises are kept, and your foreshadowings are fulfilled. Come, O Lord, quickly, hasten and do not tarry. Be born and remit the crimes of your people for neither angel nor man is able to set us free. Free us since you deigned to create us. Therefore, have compassion on us and assume our humanity to break the bonds that have held us captive for such a very long time. At one time you said, "I repent that I made man" (Genesis 6.7). Become one of us to liberate us. This liberation is indeed prefigured when the butler or cup bearer of the Pharao (Genesis 40.1–23)

is imprisoned in a dungeon and dreams of being set free. He dreams of a vine with three shoots or branches growing out of the ground. The vine does not immediately produce fruit, but rather begins to flower and then gradually produces grapes. The prisoner takes the Pharao's goblet in his hand, squeezes the juice of the grapes into it, and offers the cup to the Pharao. Later he heard a literal interpretation of this dream, indicating that after three days he would be set free. However, a mystical interpretation shows how this dream prefigures the nativity of Christ. Before the birth of the Savior, the human race was bound in wretched captivity. Finally, a vine, Christ, sprouted up from the earth, Mary. This vine has three branches representing the body, soul, and divinity of Christ, who has the power to free us from our bondage. These branches also typify the three persons of the Trinity who, likewise, have the power to free us from the diabolical dungeon. We are liberated before the Resurrection when the wine of Christ's blood is offered on the cross; and on the third day after the wine is pressed in his Passion, we finally escape from our captivity. This wine so intoxicated the Heavenly King that he forgave all our offenses. Indeed, God in his mercy has given us this wine,

Chapter 8

Figure 31. **The rod of Aaron flowers unnaturally by divine power**

Figure 32. **The sibyl sees a virgin with a child**

and instituted a daily offering under the form of a sacrament to forgive the sins of the world, for there is never an hour when God is not offended. Blessed be the divine clemency of our Savior who gives us such a remedy! Blessed be the most Blessed Virgin Mary from whom comes such a beneficial vine. When Christ was born, the vines of Engaddi (Canticle of Canticles 1.13–15) bloomed and symbolized Christ had come. Blessed be the nativity of our Savior, Jesus Christ, the source of so many benefits for angels and men! By his nativity Christ frees us from the thrall of Satan and restores the fallen to their proper place. Now that we have considered the benefits of Christ's nativity, we shall turn to the manner and the efficacy of this event. The staff of Aaron taken from an almond tree that bloomed and bore fruit by divine power prefigures the nativity. Just as this staff germinated contrary to the laws of nature, so too Mary miraculously gave birth to a son beyond the bounds of nature; the staff bore fruit without planting, but Mary gave birth to Christ without knowing man. Surely, this flowering staff shows Aaron fit to be a priest and Mary is fit to carry for us the great priest. Just as within the almond shell is the sweet meat, so also within the shell of Christ's body is hidden the divine nature.

On Aaron's staff there are green leaves, sweet flowers, and much fruit; so in Mary we find the greenness of virginity, sweetness of piety, and perpetual fruitfulness. Christ not only manifests his birth to the Jews, but he also does not hesitate to make it known to the pagans because he came to save everyone. At that time Octavius ruled the entire world and was worshiped by the Romans as they would have worshiped a god. He, nevertheless, consulted a prophet, the sibyl, to find out if there would ever be a ruler greater than himself. On the very day Christ was born in Judea, the sibyl in Rome saw in the sky a golden circle as bright as the sun. It contained a beautiful maiden holding a handsome child in her arms. The sibyl showed the emperor this vision, suggesting that a more powerful king than he himself had been born. O how powerful is the King of Kings and the Lord of Lords who has liberated the human race from the captivity of the devil! However, Augustus feared the power of this king and refused that God be revealed or called upon. O good Jesus, may we so honor your nativity and never again fall under the power of the devil!

Chapter 9

Figure 33. **The three Magi with gifts adore the child**

Figure 34. **The three Magi see a new star in the East**

In the last chapter we heard the story of the birth of Christ; let us now turn our attention to the gifts of the Magi. At the time Christ was born in Judea, his birth was announced to three kings in the East. For truly they saw a new star in the heavens in which the image of a child appeared with a golden cross shining upon his head. Then they heard a voice instructing them: "Go to Judea and there you shall find a new born king." These three kings hastened to Judea and presented their gifts to the king of Heaven. Three valiant soldiers, whom David sent to Bethlehem to bring water from a certain cistern, prefigure the Magi (2 Kings 23.15–17). The valiant soldiers did not fear the enemy's army, but courageously entered their camp, and drew the water from the cistern. Likewise, the three Magi do not fear the power of Herod, but bravely enter Judea and seek the new king. The names of the Magi are Caspar, Balthazar, and Melchior, and the names of the three soldiers are Abisai, Sobochai, and Banaias. The soldiers journey to Bethlehem for water from a cistern, but the Magi journey there for the water of eternal grace. The soldiers draw water from an earthly cistern, but the Magi receive water from the heavenly Father. Therefore, the cistern in Bethlehem prefigures the event that the heavenly cupbearer would be born in this town,

and pour the water of grace to those who thirst and freely give the water of life to those who would have a draught. King David, rejoicing in the victory of the soldiers, offers the water to God in an act of thanksgiving. Christ, King of heaven and earth, rejoices because the coming of the Magi prefigures the conversion of the pagans. David appears to have thirsted not for water but for the valor of his soldiers, and Christ thirsts for our conversion and salvation. David's soldiers journey quickly to Bethlehem and the three wise men journey there in a very short period of time. If anyone wonders how such a distance is covered in so short a period of time, it must be remembered that nothing is impossible at the birth of Christ. Whoever led Habacuc from Judea to Babylon (Daniel 14.32–38) is certainly able to lead the Magi from the East to Judea. They come to the child humbly, offering him gold, incense, and myrrh. The allegorical meaning of this offering to a new king was prefigured a long time ago during the reign of Solomon. King Solomon, although he was young, was most wise (3 Kings 2.1–9). God became an infant, and he was no less wise than he was prior to assuming human nature. Solomon while vested in garments of pure gold sat upon a most elegant ivory throne. All the kings of the earth wished to visit and bring him precious and expensive gifts. The Queen of Saba, for example, offered him many precious gifts,

Chapter 9

Figure 35. **Three soldiers bring water to King David from a cistern**

Figure 36. **The throne of Solomon**

which never before had been seen in Jerusalem. The throne of Solomon prefigures the Most Blessed Virgin Mary in whom resides Jesus Christ, true wisdom. The throne is made of the most expensive treasure, of the most radiant ivory and gold, a deep yellow beyond measure. The ivory because of its whiteness and coolness symbolizes Mary's virginity and purity, and since ivory that has aged takes on a reddish hue, one who has practiced chastity for a long time is said to be a martyr. Because gold surpasses every metal in value, it signifies chastity, the mother of every virtue. The ivory signifies Mary's purity, and her golden attire is emblematic of her perfect chastity; her charity is united inseparably to her virginity because without charity virginity is nothing in the eyes of God. Just as a thief does not fear a lamp that is not burning, so too the devil does not fear a virgin who is not charitable. The throne of Solomon is on a dais six steps above the floor, and its position prefigures how Mary surpasses the six grades of the blessed. She is above the patriarchs, prophets, and the apostles, and also above the martyrs, confessors, and the virgins. From another point of view, the six steps to the throne represent the six ages of the world, thereby showing that Mary was born into the last age. Also, 12 small lions are placed on the steps to the throne to symbolize the 12 apostles attending Mary, Queen of Heaven.

Another possible significance of the 12 lions is that they represent the 12 patriarchs, ancestors of Mary. Also the throne has two large lions representing the two tablets of the law that Mary holds fast within her heart and power. The ceiling above the throne is round because Mary is immaculate without any untidy corners. Two hands hold up the throne on both sides because God the Father and the Holy Spirit never depart from the mother of the Son. King Solomon made this throne and there was none like it in the world. Therefore, when the Magi set out upon their journey, they took such gifts that seemed to them uniquely fitting for such an infant. Gold is surely a regal gift because the nobility of the child shows he is indeed a king. Frankincense is a priestly offering, and this infant is a priest who has no equal. With myrrh it was customary in antiquity to anoint the bodies of the dead, and Christ, King and Priest, wishes to die for our salvation. We, on our part, ought to offer Christ the gold of love since he submitted to the pain of the Passion for our love, the frankincense of devout praise and thanksgiving, and finally the myrrh of compassion by the remembrance of his death. O good Jesus, may we love and sympathize with thee so that we may merit to see you in heaven!

Chapter 10

Figure 37. **Mary presents her son in the temple**

Figure 38. **The ark of the Covenant signifies Mary**

In the previous chapter we have seen how the Magi adored the Christ child; now we shall see how he is presented in the temple of the Lord. Forty days after the birth of Christ, the Blessed Virgin participates in the solemn service of the Purification. She is not obligated to undertake this ritual, for she conceived her son without man. She wishes to be purified in order to follow the law (Leviticus 12) and not be deemed a transgressor. In no way did she ever break the law because she most diligently adhered to its every prescription. On this account, the ark of the Testament that contained all the precepts of the law prefigures Mary. The ark contains the two stone tablets of Moses on which are written the ten commandments, the meaning of which we shall here explain to the reader with a brief gloss. The first commandment: You shall not adore any foreign god, but you shall love only the true God and place nothing above Him. The second: Do not take the name of God in vain and thus neither blaspheme nor unduly swear by His name. The third: Remember to keep holy the day of the Sabbath by neither sinning nor illicitly working. The fourth: Honor your father and mother by duly obeying them, helping them in necessity, and comforting them in need. The fifth: Do not kill anyone by deed, word, negligence, or thought,

not by cooperation, conspiracy, bad example, or in any other way. The sixth: Do not commit adultery in deed, thought, or in word, and do not condone any fornication where you have authority. The seventh: Do not steal nor take anything by force that does not belong to you, nor even use what the owner would not permit. The eighth: Do not swear false witness against your neighbor, and avoid all lies, wrongdoing, and slander. The ninth: Do not covet your neighbor's home, field, nor wish him any harm or injury. The tenth: Do not covet your neighbor's wife, servant or maid. These last two commandments do not overlap because the ninth pertains to immovable holdings and the tenth concerns itself with movable property. Therefore, Mary diligently observed all the commandments of God; and since the ark of the Testament contained the book of the law, this same ark prefigured Mary who read the books of the Sacred Scriptures with pleasure. Also, the rod of Aaron, which became bright with flowers at certain times, was in the ark (Numbers 17.8–10), and Mary likewise blossomed and brought forth the blessed fruit. The ark contained also a golden urn filled with manna. Further, the ark was made of incorruptible setim wood, and Mary, too, was never reduced to dust or liable to decay. The ark had four golden rings at its four corners, and Mary had the four cardinal virtues within her,

Chapter 10

Figure 39. **The candelabrum of Solomon's temple**

Figure 40. **The boy Samuel is offered to the Lord**

which are temperance, prudence, fortitude, and justice, the roots and the beginning of all the other virtues. Two golden poles are used to carry the ark, indicating the double nature of love found in Mary, love of God and love of neighbor. And finally, just as the Ark is covered with gold within and without, so also is Mary resplendent with virtue. Mary is also prefigured by the golden candlestick with seven branches that shined forth in the temple of the Lord in Jerusalem. The seven branches prefigure the seven works of mercy found in Mary: Feed the hungry, give drink to the thirsty, clothe the naked, give shelter to the homeless, visit the sick, comfort or free the prisoners, and bury the dead by providing the proper funeral rites. No one doubts that the works of mercy are found in Mary for she is indeed the mother of piety and mercy. How can a candlestick kindled by divine fire not shine; so too how can the mother of mercy not carry out the works of mercy? She is the candlestick and the flame, and she is the lamp lit by the divine light. She is full of splendor and light, she is the rosy dawn and the radiant sun. She is more radiant than all the stars; she is the moon of this world's night and the light of the angels. We honor this candlestick and candle

when we carry a lighted candle on the Feast of the Purification. After Mary offered a candle at her purification, Simeon prophesied that her son is the light of revelation. Christ, the son of Mary, is the lighted candle and this candle has three parts: fire, light, and wax. In Christ there are three parts: body, spirit, and divinity. This candle is offered to the Lord for the human race to illumine our dark night. The offering of this most blessed and glorious candle is prefigured in the child, Samuel (1 Kings 1.5–28). Because Anna, wife of Elcana, did not have any children, she shed copious tears and prayed to God for a son. God gave Anna a son contrary to nature just as He gave a son to Mary above the power of nature. Anna called her son Samuel and offered him to the Lord God; Mary named her son Jesus and offered him to his true Father. Anna dedicated her son to be a champion of the people, whereas Mary dedicated her son to shield the world from danger. Finally, her own people opposed the son of Anna, and the son of Mary is condemned to the most shameful death. Simeon indeed had predicted that a sword would pierce the heart of Mary (Luke 2.35). O good Jesus, may your Presentation be so venerated that we may merit to dwell with you in the heavenly temple in the company of the angels.

Chapter 11

Figure 41. *All the idols fall to the ground when Jesus enters Egypt*

Figure 42. *The Egyptians make a statue of a virgin with an infant*

In the last chapter we have learned how Jesus was presented in the temple, and now let us consider how he flees into Egypt. When King Herod sought to kill the Christ child, Joseph, forewarned by an angel, escapes with Mary and the infant to Egypt (Matthew 2.13), and immediately after the Holy Family enters the land of the Pharao, all their idols and statues fall from their pedestals. In ancient times Jeremias prophesied this event to the Egyptians (Jeremias 43.13) when they had led him into captivity. After the Egyptians had learned that Jeremias was a prophet, they inquired whether any marvelous events would happen in their land. Jeremias responded that in the distant future a maiden would give birth and all the statues of their gods and all their idols would fall and break. The Egyptians concluded that this child is more powerful than their gods, and they discussed among themselves how they might honor him. Therefore, they carved a statue of a maiden with a most handsome infant and honored the child according to their custom. Long after this event, Ptolemy asked them why they had acted in this way, and they responded that they are waiting for the fulfillment of a prophecy. This prophecy that the holy Jeremias proclaimed is indeed fulfilled when Christ enters Egypt with his mother, for then all the statues and idols of the Egyptian gods are dashed to the ground. The Egyptians then told Ptolemy that a virgin, as foretold, had given birth to a son. Further, the birth of the Christ child is also prefigured when Moses shattered the Pharao's crown. The Pharao had a regal crown

on which an artisan skillfully crafted the god, Amon. Because it was prophesied to the Egyptians that a Jewish child would be born who would liberate his people and overcome the Egyptians, the Pharao therefore ordered the Jews to cast their infants into the river (Exodus 1.22) so that the one they feared would be killed. Amram and Jocabeth decided to live apart because they would rather be childless than to kill their child after birth. However, they received a sign from God to live together because the Egyptians would fear their child. Finally, Jocabeth conceived and brought forth a handsome son whom she hid within her home for three months. When she was no longer able to conceal the child, she put him in a small basket and placed it near the river. At about the same time the Pharao's daughter walked by, found the infant, named him Moses, and vowed to rear the child. Later she decided to present the young boy to the Pharao, who immediately began to play with him and placed his crown upon the boy's head. Moses threw the crown to the floor and shattered it completely. When an Egyptian high priest saw this, he exclaimed, "This is the child Amon ordered us to kill," and drawing his sword he was poised to slay the boy. However, other courtiers said the child had only acted foolishly, and, to prove their point, they gave hot coals to Moses, who on a command from God put them in his mouth.

Chapter 11

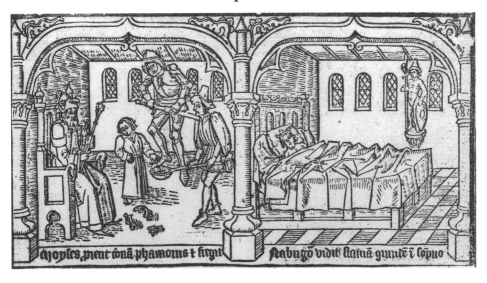

*Figure 43. **Moses throws down the Pharao's crown and shatters it***

*Figure 44. **Nabuchodonosor sees a large statue in a dream***

Moses is saved by the power of God so he could later lead the Jews out of Egyptian slavery. What is said here about Moses agrees figuratively with the Christ child. King Pharao had ordered the Jews to drown all their children hoping to drown Moses at the same time. Likewise, King Herod ordered that all the infants of Bethlehem be killed, hoping to kill Jesus with the others. Just as an act of God saves Moses from death at the hands of the Pharao, so too Jesus is saved from the sword of Herod by divine intervention. Moses is born to lead the children of Israel out of Egypt, and Christ became man to free us from Hell. Moses shattered the image of the god on the Pharao's crown, and Jesus reduced all the statues of the idols and gods of Egypt to worthless fragments. A statue that King Nabuchodonosor saw in a dream suggests the destruction of the idols (Daniel 2.1–49). The head and neck of this statue are made of gold; its arms and chest are made of silver; the stomach and thighs are brass; the legs appear to be iron; the feet are partly clay, and the other parts of the statue seem to be iron. A stone cut out of a mountain without the help of a human hand struck the feet of the statue and crushed and reduced it to dust.

Afterward, the stone grew into a large mountain. This stone is a figure of the Son of God, Jesus Christ, who came into this world for the salvation of humankind. Further, this stone is cut from the mountain without the help of human hands, just as Christ is born of Mary without human assistance. This stone or Christ crushes all the idols of Egypt, even if they are gold or silver, brass or iron, and he also shatters those made of clay. All these materials are in the previously mentioned statues that were toppled despite how they were made. The stone, after it crushed the statue, grew into a huge mountain, just as the faith in Jesus Christ spread throughout the world and destroyed idolatry. As the stone grew in size to become a huge mountain, so too the enemies of Christ, such as Herod, are diminished in size and are almost reduced to nothing. When Christ returns to Judea, he grows in age and wisdom before God and man; he grows into a mountain of such greatness and size that he fills the heavens and the earth. "Whoever ascends the mountain of the Lord, and whoever has clean hands and a pure heart shall see Christ here, shall receive the blessing of the Lord now, and later receive the mercy of his salvation" (Psalm 23.3–5). O, good Jesus, give us a pure heart to serve you, and after ascending the mountain we shall behold you for all eternity.

Chapter 12

Figure 45. **John baptizes Jesus in the Jordan**

Figure 46. **Those entering the temple wash in a bronze laver**

In the chapter we have just finished, we have seen how the Holy Family fled to Egypt; now let us consider how John baptizes Christ in the Jordan. When Christ began his thirtieth year, he journeys to the Jordan river so that John may baptize him. The Son of the Living God does not need baptism but participates for our salvation. Also, Christ wishes to impart a power to the water by the touch of his body, so that a newly baptized person thus cleansed may enter the kingdom of heaven. This event is prefigured in ancient times by the brazen sea, a ritual purification fount, placed at the entrance to the temple at Jerusalem (3 Kings 7.23–27). The priests about to enter the temple are obliged to wash in this fount, just as everyone who wishes to enter the heavenly temple of the Lord must first be cleansed through baptism. We must note that there are many types of baptism, namely by water, blood, and by fire; baptism in the river is through immersion in water, by blood through the suffering of martyrdom, and by fire through the Holy Spirit. If a person dies with the intention to be baptized later with water, then the baptism by fire is sufficient. If the person survives, then the intention alone is not sufficient, for the person must still receive baptism with water. Likewise, baptism by blood is not valid if one does not have the intention to receive later baptism with water. Therefore, baptism with water is most necessary,

for those wishing to enter the celestial temple of the Lord. Baptism must be performed with pure water, not wine, not milk, nor any other liquid. The brazen sea or ritual cleansing fount, was skillfully manufactured by blending different metals, just as the ritual of baptism is recited in many different languages and follows an approved form. Anyone may confer baptism if he or she intends to abide by and implement the practice approved by the Church. Twelve oxen support the brazen fount and prefigure the 12 apostles who spread baptism throughout the world. We must not fail to mention that there is a mirror above this ritual-cleansing fount so that those entering the temple may examine themselves for any defilement. This examination prefigures the perfection of conscience that baptism requires, the hatred of sin, penance, and a contrite heart. John the Baptist thus addressed the Pharisees when he saw them coming to be baptized without contrition of heart, "Brood of vipers! How will you flee the wrath of the judge about to come! You who receive baptism and do not have any contrition in your heart!" (Matthew 3.7). Whoever receives baptism with a contrite heart is cleansed of all defilement from his or her sins. This cleansing is prefigured in ancient times by Naaman the Syrian, a leper, who is made clean in the river Jordan in a most extraordinary way (4 Kings 5.1–14).

Chapter 12

Figure 47. **The leper Naaman [bathes] seven times and is cleansed**

Figure 48. **The Jordan is dry for the crossing of the children of God**

Naaman is a heathen and of course does not know God, but, nevertheless, he goes to the prophet of God, Eliseus, for a cure. Eliseus orders Naaman to bathe in the Jordan River seven times, thus being cleansed of all his leprosy. The command to bathe seven times in the river prefigures the washing away of the seven deadly sins in baptism. Just as the waters of the Jordan made the flesh of Naaman look like that of a small child, so also baptism makes the sinner as pure as an infant. If the infant were to die before he had the occasion to sin again, he would enter the Kingdom of Heaven immediately. This truth is indicated when the heavens opened above Christ after John had baptized him in the Jordan. Therefore whoever wishes to enter the Kingdom of Heaven shall not enter unless he or she is baptized. This truth was prefigured a long time ago at the crossing of the Jordan when the children of Israel entered the promised land. Now everyone who wishes to enter the true promised land must pass through the baptismal fount. The children of Israel carried the ark of the Lord to the middle of the Jordan and placed it there; then all the people with their cattle crossed over. The water above the ark did not cascade down, but amassed itself together like a huge mountain while the water beneath the ark rushed out to sea,

and the bed of the Jordan remained dry (Josue 3.15–17). Next the Israelites carried 12 stones from the bed of the river to make a mound to be a lasting memorial where the ark had stood. After the people had crossed the bed of the Jordan with dry feet, the river bed returned to the way it was before. The ark of the Testament, which had stood in the middle of the river bed, prefigured Christ who was baptized in the same river. The ark contained the rod of Aaron that had blossomed in ancient times and the flower of this staff prefigures Christ. In the ark was manna, the bread of heaven, and Christ is the living bread who descended from heaven. In the ark was Deuteronomy, the book of the law, and the same God, now made man, gave this law to the Jews. In the ark are the tablets of the ten commandments, and the same God who gave us these precepts now institutes baptism. The ark was made of wood, incorruptible setim, and the body of Christ is incorruptible although he died and was buried. The ark, though made of wood, was covered with the finest gold, and the mantle of Christ's deity covered him in death as well as in life. Finally, the 12 stones prefigure the testimony of the 12 apostles who preached the baptism of Christ throughout the world. O, good Jesus, may we so venerate your baptism that we may merit to dwell with you in perpetual glory.

Chapter 13

Figure 49. **Christ is tempted by the devil in three different ways**

Figure 50. **Daniel destroys Bel and kills the dragon**

In the last chapter we heard how John baptized Christ; let us now consider how he is tempted by the devil. After his baptism, Jesus, inspired by the Holy Spirit, journeys into the desert. He is not transported through the air as an angel carried the prophet Habacuc to Babylon (Daniel 14.32–38), and, likewise, the devil did not carry him to the top of the temple. The word to lead (ducere) is not always synonymous with the word to carry (bajulare). One meaning of the word to lead (ducere) is to guide or command as in the sentence: Moses led the children of Israel out of Egypt. This sentence does not mean that Moses carried them on his back. The devil does not carry Christ through the air, but rather appears to him in the form of a man to persuade him with a convincing argument. Christ wishes to undergo the temptations for us, and he goes up to the top of the temple and ascends the mountain (Matthew 4.1–10). Christ allows himself to be tempted for our instruction to show that no one is able to live in this world without experiencing temptation. No one should think it possible to live without temptation, for if we escape one, the devil immediately prepares another assault. This is the reason Christ is tempted three times. If God had not given us a guardian angel, we would surely be unable to overcome these temptations.

Just as the rays of the sun appear to be filled with specks of dust, so too the world is filled with demons. If we see anyone who is tempted and falls, we should have compassion for him in our hearts. We should neither condemn nor make public the sinner's plight, and we ought to conceal and excuse the sin. If we are unable to excuse the sin, we shall excuse the intention to the extent we are able. If we are unable to excuse either the sin or the intention, we should lament the fact and think, "O how many more wretched things might happen to me if God did not mercifully protect me." We must remember Satan tempted Christ with three vices: gluttony, pride, and avarice. Since Jesus had fasted 40 days and 40 nights, Satan suspected he would be hungry. Satan ordinarily tempts a person by the sin to which, he feels, the individual is most inclined. So when he was sure that Jesus was famished, he decided to tempt him with gluttony just as he tempted Adam. He felt confident that one desirous of food will most likely fall into gluttony, rather than abstain. On this account, Satan tempted the first parents and urged them to eat the forbidden fruit. We struggle in vain to overcome this vice

Chapter 13

Figure 51. **David overcomes Goliath, the Philistine**

Figure 52. **David kills a bear and a lion**

unless we first learn to curb gluttony and immoderation. Daniel, when he overthrew the idol Bel and the dragon, prefigures Christ's victory over Satan and the first temptation (Daniel 14.1–26). In Babylon the idol Bel is worshiped as a god and each day his priests offer him a large amount of food and drink, loaves of bread made of 12 measures of flour, 6 jars of wine, and the carcasses of 40 roasted sheep. At night the priests with their families enter this area of the temple by a secret passage to feast on the food offered to Bel. The next day, Daniel found the footprints of the priests and their kin in the ashes that he had scattered over the floor. The king ordered the idol destroyed and the intruders put to death. In the same place a dragon lurked in a cave, and all the people thought it a god. The priests fed the dragon daily, but it never left the cave. Daniel, with the permission of the king, made a ball of pitch, grease, and hair and thrust it into the dragon's mouth. Upon eating, the beast burst asunder. Daniel, who destroyed these ravenous creatures, prefigures Christ who conquered the temptation of gluttony. Further, Christ outwitted Satan and overcame the temptation of pride. David prefigures this victory when he slew Goliath a long time ago. Goliath boasted most arrogantly of his strength, and thought there was no equal to him among the children of Israel.

David brought Goliath down to the ground with his sling, and with the help of God slew him with his own sword. The proud giant is a figure of Lucifer who aspired to be like God; David, the shepherd, prefigured Christ who humbly overcame the temptation of pride. Temptations of pride are diverse and are found everywhere, not only in the world, but in the cloister too. Often the person who is free of all vices succumbs to vainglory and desires to be praised. Often pride lies hidden in one clothed in the most humble garments just as it is found under the gilded purple robes of a king. Finally, Christ defeats the devil the third time in the temptation of avarice. David also prefigures this event when he slew the lion and the bear, conventional symbols of avarice because of their penchant for stealing sheep. David rescues his sheep and kills the thieves just as Christ, victorious over the temptation of avarice, expels the devil from his presence. After Satan is defeated, angels come to attend to Christ, the victor. Therefore, whoever fights courageously triumphs over Satan and is worthy of the aid and fellowship of the holy angels. O, good Jesus, grant us victory in every temptation so we may merit to dwell in your eternal glory.

Chapter 14

*Figure 53. **Magdalen repents in the house of Simon***

*Figure 54. **Manasses does penance in captivity***

In the previous chapter we have learned how Satan tempted Christ; let us now consider how he healed Mary Magdalen. When Christ began his thirtieth year, he is baptized by John and tempted by the devil. Later, Christ himself begins to administer baptism and to preach to the people, showing them the way to salvation by example and teaching. When he began to preach, he uttered these inspiring words, "Do penance, for the Kingdom of God is at hand" (Matthew 4.17), and then he mercifully preached about the opening of the heavenly kingdom. No one ever heard such words before, true words indeed and worthy of acceptance by everyone. The malicious sinner may merit the kingdom of heaven through penance, and this truth becomes apparent in the life of Mary Magdalen who possessed seven demons, the seven deadly sins. These deadly sins were cast out of her by contrition and penance, and she mercifully obtained God's clemency (Luke 8.2). No sinner should despair of God's mercy because He is ever present to release the debts of every penitent. As mentioned above, He promises every penitent the kingdom of heaven that had been impossible to achieve. King Manasses, who repeatedly offended God by killing His prophets and by reckoning Him to be nothing, prefigures this type of forgiveness (4 Kings 21.1–17). Manasses tortured so many men of God who denounced him

that the streets of Jerusalem became purple with the blood of the prophets. The holy prophet Isaias, who rebukes the king because of his sins, is cut in half with a saw. After Manasses had committed many sins, he was captured by his enemies, led into exile, and cast into prison. While he was incarcerated he became contrite, deplored his sins from the bottom of his heart, and prayed to the Lord with profuse and bitter tears. "I have sinned," he lamented, "more than the number of grains of sand by the sea and I am not worthy to see the heights of heaven. Because of the number of my iniquities, I have provoked your wrath, O most merciful God, sinned before you, and I have broken your laws." The merciful Lord extended to him His clemency, mercifully accepted his penance, freed him from prison and captivity, and restored him to His kingdom in Jerusalem. Manasses is a symbol of an evil sinner who sins without fear and does not believe in God and tortures the servants of the Lord after he refuses to heed their admonitions. While such an individual perseveres in mortal sin, he remains a prisoner of the devil; but if he becomes truly sorry for his offenses, the merciful Lord is eager to rescue him.

Chapter 14

Figure 55. *The father and master of the house welcomes the prodigal son*

Figure 56. **Admonished for adultery, David repents**

The Lord taught this lesson in a parable when he told the story of the prodigal son found in the Gospel of Luke (15.11–32). The son leaves his father's home and journeys to a far off country where he squanders all his wealth by living luxuriously. Destitute, he comes to a farm belonging to one of the townsmen who employs him to feed his swine. This prodigal son represents the sinner who turns away from his heavenly home, then dwells in a distant land. According to the prophet, salvation is far distant from the sinner. The sinner squanders his wealth, turns his senses and talents to malice, belongs to the townsman, Lucifer, whose swine he tends and whose devils he feeds with his sins. The prodigal son reaches such a state of deprivation that he has only husks to eat, and because of the extremity of his poverty, he finally begins to do penance. In this transformation we see the mercy of the Savior at work who urges sinners to do penance. The Lord seeks and delights so much in our salvation that he uses whatever means necessary to influence us. Some he attracts by inspiration, but others he persuades by salvific preaching. Some he influences by bestowing benefices,

but others he motivates by flagellation. This latter method, penance, influenced the prodigal son to return to his father's home. When the father sees his son approaching from a distance, he runs to him, embraces and kisses him on the cheek, just as the Lord hastens to the penitent with grace, mercifully receives him, and forgives all his sins. King David prefigured this type of forgiveness a long time ago when he committed adultery and homicide against Urias (2 Kings 12.1–23). When Nathan reproached David for his crimes, David responded, "I have sinned." God was ready to forgive David immediately and Nathan answered, "The Lord has taken away your sin, and it is forgiven." O how great is your love, O Lord, O how ineffable! You do not disdain any sinner, whatever his state! You did not reject Peter, Paul, Thomas, and Matthew, David, Achab, Manasses, the thief, Achior and Zachaeus, Ninive, the Samaritan woman, Rahab, Ruth, and the woman taken in adultery, Theophilus, Gilbert, Thaiden, and Mary the Egyptian, the Eunuch, Simon, Cornelius, and Ezechias, Magdalen, Longinus, and Mary sister of Moses. Therefore, we should not despair because of the enormity of our sins, for we have the testimony of our divine mercy. O, good Jesus, grant us true and perfect contrition so that we may merit to come into your presence.

Chapter 15

Figure 57. **Christ weeps over the city of Jerusalem**

Figure 58. **Jeremias laments over Jerusalem**

In the last chapter we heard about the conversion of Mary Magdalen; now let us consider what happened to Christ on Palm Sunday. On that day three notable events take place, which are prefigured in the past. Jesus weeps when he sees the city of Jerusalem, is received with honor and praise by the citizens of the city, and he casts the merchants out of the temple. First, when Jesus sees Jerusalem, he weeps, for he feels pity and compassion for the misery about to befall the city. The tears of our Lord and Savior are prefigured in the Lamentations of Jeremias who bemoaned the desolation of Jerusalem caused by the Babylonians. Now Jesus laments the destruction of the city about to be caused by the Romans. Following the example of Christ, we ought to be moved to compassion when we see our neighbors suffering. It is better to have compassion for the unfortunate than to give alms, for when we show pity we give something of ourselves to the destitute. Further, we ought to show kindness to those who harm us, following the example of Christ who had compassion for his enemies. It is impossible not to merit mercy and grace if we are sincerely kind to the distressed. The second notable event that happens on Palm Sunday is the honor and praise the people show Christ upon his entry into Jerusalem. The songs of praise and honor King David received after he slew Goliath prefigure this event (1 Kings 17.50–58; 18.7); in their canticle the singers preferred David to Saul,

singing that Saul killed 1,000 but David 10,000. David who overcame Goliath, namely the devil, our adversary, prefigured our Lord Jesus Christ. On Palm Sunday this true David, Christ, is honored in many different ways when the people greet him. Some shout, "Hosanna to the Son of David," others call out, "Blessed is he who comes in the name of the Lord." Some proclaim that he is the King of Israel, others sing prophetically that he is the Savior of the world. Some run before him with flowers, some with palms, while others spread their garments along his way. The mystical meaning of the word "Jerusalem" is vision of peace, and the name also spiritually means the truly faithful. Our Savior is prepared to come to us at any hour, and we, contrite, must hasten to meet him. We sing praises to the Lord in voices of acclamation when we woefully recite our sins in confession. We carry branches of palms in our hands to praise God when we discipline our bodies for the satisfaction of our sins. We strew our garments along the way to honor God when we give alms to the poor of Christ. We run to the Lord with flowers and honor him when we offer praise by works of mercy and virtuous acts. We bless Christ Jesus who comes in the name of the Lord

Chapter 15

Figure 59. **David is welcomed with praise**

Figure 60. **Heliodorus is scourged**

when we thank him for all his blessings. We declare publicly that he is our king and Lord when we perform all our work with reverence and fear of God. The third notable event that happens on Palm Sunday is that Jesus makes a scourge of little cords of rope and drives the merchants and their customers from the temple (John 2.13–16). He overturns the tables of the money changers and scatters their coins, for they are usurers and bankers representing the Pharisees. This scourging by the Lord is prefigured by Heliodorus whom King Seleuceus orders to go to Jerusalem to plunder the riches of the temple (2 Machabees 3). When Heliodorus boldly enters the temple of the Lord with an armed guard, he immediately provokes the vengeance of God, and a frightful horse with a rider armed and dreadful appears unexpectedly before him. The horse strikes Heliodorus with his two front hooves, knocks him to the floor, holds him there with much snorting and neighing. Two exceedingly strong young men appear and scourge him to within a breath of his life. After they finish, the young men and the horse disappear, and the beaten Heliodorus remains motionless as if he were dead. However, the chief priest prays for him and Heliodorus arises, returns home to his lord and reports, "If the king has an enemy he wants to put to death, send the foe to Jerusalem to plunder the temple" (2 Machabees 3.38).

Heliodorus is beaten because he is about to steal from the temple, and in the New Testament, the merchants lose their money because of usury. The Pharisees placed the money changers and bankers in the temple to lend money to those wishing to make an offering. They are obliged by law not to make a profit, but they did receive small gifts, figs, grapes, nuts, and fruit, almonds, chickens, geese, doves, and the like. They cleverly covered their usury with a cloak, and paid no heed to the word of the Lord written by Ezechiel, "Do not accept usury or a profit" (18.8). Dear brethren, commit Ezechiel's words to memory! How sad it is! Today there are many Christians in the Church who cleverly cloak their usury. They do not make loans motivated by the love of God, but rather are influenced by a profit, services, favors or promotions. These people sin grievously, forgetting the words of the Lord, "Lend, hoping for nothing thereby" (Luke 6.35). The Lord will drive such sinners from the church and will banish them from the land of the living. Let us be zealous about the Church and our religion unless we wish to be perpetually scourged. Let us give up usury and any hope for a profit so that we are not cast out of the temple of glory by the Lord. O, good Jesus, teach us to be vigilant so that we may merit the temple of glory for all eternity.

Chapter 16

Figure 61. **Christ eats the Paschal lamb with his disciples**

Figure 62. **Manna is given to the children of Israel in the desert**

In the last chapter we heard what happened on Palm Sunday; now we shall learn about the Last Supper and the sacrament of the Eucharist. As the time grew near when he was willing to suffer his Passion, Christ decided to institute the sacrament of communion as an everlasting memorial, and to prove to us his love when he gives of himself in the form of food. The manna that was given to the Israelites while they were in the desert prefigures the Eucharist. Great is the love the Lord showed to his people, but infinitely greater is the love he bestows upon us. To the Israelites he gives a bread limited by time and matter; to us he gives a bread that is eternal and that transcends the material. Manna is called the bread from heaven, but truly it never was from heaven since God created it in the air or the sky. Christ our Savior is the true living bread who descends from heaven to be our food. God gives only a figure of the true bread to the Israelites, but to us he gives a divine bread, not a figure. Manna has many different figurative meanings that are completely fulfilled in the Sacred Eucharist. Manna is a marvel of nature, for it melts in the rays of the sun yet hardens in fire. Likewise, the Eucharist melts and disappears in the heart of the proud, but abides and knows not how to depart from a heart on fire with divine love. The wicked receive the Eucharist for their damnation,

but the good receive it for divine and everlasting consolation. Whenever manna descended from the sky, dew fell with it, signifying that grace accompanies the Eucharist. Manna is as white as snow, signifying that whoever receives communion must have a heart pure and clean. Manna has in itself all the delights of earthly food (Wisdom 16.20), but the Eucharist has the delights of heavenly food. This heavenly taste, which is not perceived as one consumes the sacrament, is realized only in holy meditation and contemplation. The taste of manna changes to accommodate each individual, but nothing in this world can compare to the sweetness of the sacrament of the Eucharist. Whoever might taste this bliss but once would count all the delights of the world to be worthless. Peter, who tasted this joy on Mount Tabor (Matthew 17.1–4), immediately wished to build tabernacles and to remain there. Moses commanded every one of his followers to go out each morning before sunrise to collect only one omer of manna for the day. It happened miraculously that the greedy who collected more than one omer had only one when they returned home, and those unable to collect a full measure had a full omer when they returned home. The communicant who receives several hosts does not have more than he who receives only one, and he who receives only a portion of a host does not have less than he who receives a complete one or even several.

Chapter 16

Figure 63. **The Jews eat the Paschal lamb**

Figure 64. **Melchisedech offers bread and wine to Abraham**

The eating of the Paschal Lamb on Thursday, the day before the preparation for the Sabbath, prefigures the Last Supper. The Lord commanded the Israelites to eat the lamb when they were liberated from captivity in Egypt, and Christ instituted the sacrament of the Eucharist to free us from the power of the devil. When the Israelites eat the Paschal Lamb, they gird their garments with a cincture, hold staffs in their hands, and stand. Communicants must also be girded with chastity of mind and body, hold the staff of faith firmly in their hands, and stand erect in the good life they are beginning, never again falling into the mire they are about to leave. The lamb is eaten with wild and bitter lettuce, and we must receive the body of the Lord with bitter contrition. Those who partake in the Paschal Lamb must shod their feet, for the feet, according to holy Scripture, symbolize pleasure; the communicants must shod their feet to protect themselves because their desires may be defiled by any uncleanness. The Paschal Lamb is not boiled in water, but roasted by fire, and the communicants should burn with the fire of charity to receive the sacrament worthily. Christ gives us the Eucharist under the form of bread and wine, and this was prefigured a long time ago by the king and priest Melchisedech (Genesis 14. 18–20). Four kings laid waste to the land where Abraham had dwelt, captured many spoils, and led away Lot with many other captives. However, Abraham followed them with his servants, overwhelmed them and returned home with all the captives. Melchisedech runs to meet Abraham and offers him bread and wine that prefigures the divine sacrament. Melchisedech, a king and priest of the most high God, is a sign or figure for our Lord Jesus Christ; for Christ is indeed the king who created every kingdom and he is the priest who celebrated the first mass. Melchisedech offers bread and wine, but Christ instituted this sacrament under the form of bread and wine. Why is a priest said to be of the order of Melchisedech? Because this sacrament is prefigured by his offering, and he is an apt model of priestly dignity. A priest may well be called a regal prince since he surpasses in dignity imperial princes, excels in power the patriarchs, prophets, and even the power of the angels. The priest can consecrate the sacrament that neither patriarchs, prophets, or angels can do. The Son of God is born of Mary but once, but the priest changes bread into the body of Christ many times, and because of this sacrament we must honor the priest whom Christ has deemed worthy for ordination. O, good Jesus, give us your sacrament to worship so that we may never be separated from you.

Chapter 17

Figure 65. **Christ fells his enemies with one word**

Figure 66. **Samson fells a thousand with the jawbone of an ass**

In the chapter that has gone before we have learned how Christ instituted the Eucharist; now we shall learn in this chapter how he meets his enemies. After Judas had received communion with the other disciples, he departed to meet with the enemies of Christ. O how great is the kindness and mercy of Christ! O how great is the malice and folly of Judas! Christ nourishes him with the sacrament of his body and blood, but Judas had already betrayed him in his heart. Christ, all knowing, still would not expose Judas nor deny him the sacrament, and, in so doing, he shows a priest how to distribute communion. A priest who knows that a person has committed a deadly sin must neither deny that person communion nor defame him. Now, Judas goes to meet the enemies of Christ, and Jesus departs for a place where he knows he will meet them. The enemies arrive and are armed with swords and cudgels, seeking him in the dark with lamps and firebrands. Jesus for his part comes to the meeting place unarmed and gently seeks out those who are seeking him. They stand before him as giants asking if he is Jesus of Nazareth. Jesus answers most kindly, speaking in a humble voice, "I am." When the rabble heard these words, all stepped back, and fell to the ground as though they were dead. O foolish enemies of Christ! What good is accomplished to come in such numbers,

and all are thrown to the ground by one gentle word! To what profit are your many devices and schemes that are brought to nil by a single word? To what profit are your frightening arms that are rendered useless by one word? Do you not see that Christ alone is more powerful than all of you? If he were willing to kill you, would he not have been able to do so? Assuredly, he might have commanded the earth to open under your feet and swallow all of you alive as Dathan and Abiron were swallowed (Numbers 16.30). He might have rained fire and brimstone to destroy you as Sodom and Gomorrha were destroyed (Genesis 19.24). He might have destroyed all with rain from heaven as he did to the entire world a long time ago (Genesis 6). He might have changed you into a rock as he did to Lot's wife (Genesis 19.26), or make you suffer the plagues the Egyptians suffered (Exodus 7–14). He might have changed everyone into dust as he did to Sennacherib's army of 180,000 men (4 Kings 19.35), or he might have killed you suddenly as he killed the sons of Juda, Her and Onan (Genesis 38.7–10). He might have killed you by the sword of an angel as he slew many during the reign of David (2 Kings 24.15–16). He might have given you over to the power of the devil as he gave the seven husbands of Sara during the time of Tobias (Tobias 6.14). He might have sent fire to destroy you as he did to Korah with his 250 men (Numbers 16.35),

Chapter 17

Figure 67. **Samgar kills 600 men with a ploughshare**

Figure 68. **David kills 800 men with his attack**

or he might have sent fire serpents as he did to your ancestors when they had spoken against him. He might have sent a lion on the prowl to tear you to pieces as he did to those colonists in Samaria under King Salamanasar (4 Kings 17.24–26). He might have a fierce bear tear you apart as he did to the 40 boys who laughed at Eliseus (4 Kings 2.24). He might have beaten and trampled upon you as he did to Heliodorus (2 Machabees 3.24–27), or he might have put you to death with decay and worms as he did to Antioclus (2 Machabees 9.5–10). He might have struck you unexpectedly with leprosy as he once struck Giezi (4 Kings 5.20–27), and the sister of Moses Mary (Numbers 12.1–10). He might have struck you with blindness as he struck the Syrian army during the time of Eliseus (4 Kings 6.8–18), or he might have made your arms wither as he once did to king Jeroboam in Bethel near the altar (3 Kings 13.4). Finally, he might have consumed your weapons with worms as he consumed all the bow strings of the Syrian army. He could have done all these things had he so wished, but he only wishes to cast you down for a little while. He acts accordingly to show how freely he chooses death, for if he wishes to resist, you could neither seize nor hold him. Therefore, after Christ shows his power, he gives his adversaries permission to get up and to gain control of themselves. Christ's victory over his enemies, which we have now described, is prefigured in Samson, Samgar, and David. Samson fell 1,000 men with the jawbone of an ass,

and Samgar kills 600 with a ploughshare. If these men are able to overcome so many adversaries with the help of God, it is no marvel that all the enemies fell before Christ. Scripture calls King David, who killed 800 men in one charge, a most tender wood worm (2 Kings 23.8). The wood worm, when it is touched, appears to be very soft, but when it touches, it bores through the hardest wood. No one is milder than David when he is with his household, but with his enemies no one is harder in judgment than he. Likewise, Christ is the most gentle and patient person in this world, but he will be most severe in his judgment of his enemies. He lived a gentle, quiet life, walks about unarmed, but is treated vilely as it is plaintively lamented in the Psalms, "I am a worm and no man" (Psalms 21.7). However, he is indeed a wood worm because his enemies executed him on wood of a cross. He is fittingly called the most tender because his flesh is most tender and noble, and to the extent that he is tender and noble, his passion and suffering are most harsh and cruel. Rightfully, he cries out in the words of the Lamentations to all those who pass by the way to see if they have ever witnessed such punishment. O, good Jesus, grant us to see your bitter sorrow that we may merit to live and rejoice with you in the Kingdom of Heaven.

52

Chapter 18

*Figure 69. **Christ is deceitfully betrayed***

*Figure 70. **Joab kills his brother, Amasa***

In the last chapter we heard how Christ cast his enemies to the ground; let us now consider how Judas greets him deceitfully. Judas, the betrayer of our Savior, gives the enemies of Christ a signal — a kiss, a wicked and malicious sign beyond measure. A kiss has always been construed as a sign of love, but wicked Judas changes it to a sign of betrayal. This wicked salutation so deceitfully given to Christ was prefigured a long time ago when Joab greeted Amasa, feigning trust and calling him brother just as Judas greets Christ with a malicious intent and calls him Master. Joab took Amasa's chin with his right hand to kiss him, but with his left hand drew his dagger to kill him. Judas, likewise, seems to hold Christ's chin with his right hand and says courteously, "Hail Master." However, it appears that he draws a dagger with his left hand to stab Christ because we read that his insidious act is hidden by flattering words. O, Judas, why do you betray your Savior? What makes you so malicious that you wish to oppose him? He did give you the honor and dignity. Why do you vent such malice against him? He did choose you to be an apostle over and above the 72 disciples. Compared to the others you are the most deceitful. He numbered you among his 12 most special friends, but you deserted him to join his enemies. He admitted you to his secrets along with the other apostles,

but you repeatedly make secret plans against him with his enemies. He sent you out to preach without sack or wallet, and wherever you went, you lacked nothing because of his care. Unmindful of his thoughtfulness you now come to betray him for such a small amount of money. He gave you power to heal the sick, but you plotted to bind him and make him infirm. He gave you power to cast out devils, but you betray him into the hands of his enemies. He made you his bursar and steward, but you make yourself his adversary and traitor. He puts you in charge of the money collected for him in the form of alms. Since you have the authority to use this money, why do you sell your Lord for such a small amount? You stole as much as you pleased from the coffers of your God, so why do you now sell him for 30 pieces of silver? He deemed you worthy to eat his most Holy Body, but you do not fear to sell his body to his enemies to be put to death. He gave you his most sacred blood to drink, yet you do not fear to betray him and to shed his blood. He was not ashamed to minister to you and to wash your feet, and you are not ashamed to salute him so deceitfully. He was not unwilling even to kiss you, but then your corrupt heart perseveres in its malice.

Chapter 18

Figure 71. **King Saul gives David evil in return for goodness**

Figure 72. **Cain deceitfully kills his brother, Abel**

When you greeted him with evil intent, he calls you his friend, and even this kindness does not change you. He did not tell your betrayal to Peter and the other apostles because he knew they would strike you down, and he wished to prevent this from happening. In the Old Law it is written, "a tooth for a tooth and an eye for an eye" (Exodus 21.24; Leviticus 24.20). Never is it permitted to return evil for good, but Judas, this is just what you do, betraying such kindness. Likewise your confederates, the enemies of Christ, also return evil for good because they crucify the Savior. Saul prefigured both you, Judas, and also the enemies of Christ because he never ceased to return evil for good to David. Even after David became Saul's son-in-law, Saul immediately plotted his murder. In the same manner, the Son of God assumes our human nature, and you, Judas, assemble an armed band to kill him. David overcame Saul's dreaded enemy, Goliath, but Saul sets a deadly snare for David just as one would do to an enemy. God repeatedly overcame all your enemies, and now, because of your madness, you oppose him. Many times David puts to flight the evil spirit from Saul, and in return Saul brandishes his lance to kill him. Often your Savior called you from idolatry, but now you arm for his death. Always at the king's bidding, David is either coming or going,

but Saul always plots his death. Christ walked about the countryside, teaching the way to the truth, and you seek to strike him down, one who always served you and never harmed you. David soothes Saul's grief by playing the cithara, but Saul always wishes to inflict pain or death upon him. Christ healed the sick and revived the dead, but now you and your followers arm to kill him. You are like Cain who murdered his brother without cause, a brother who did no harm, but yet was killed. The brother's sacrificial gift pleased God, and that is the reason, if it may be called a reason, why Cain killed Abel. In the same manner, Christ pleases the people and God, but you said, "If we let him alone, all will believe in him" (John 11.48). If all the world believes him, who then would be against him? Was not everything he taught true and useful? Cain greets his brother with flattery but then kills him with a terrible blow. Judas greets Christ pleasantly but then deceitfully hands him over to his enemies to be killed. Cain killed his brother, but Judas and the enemies of Christ kill their brother and their father, for Christ is our father who created us, and he is our brother who adopted our human nature. O good Jesus, who deems to become our brother, have mercy on us and protect us as our merciful Father.

Chapter 19

Figure 73. *Christure is blindfolded, spit upon, and beaten*

Figure 74. *Miriam's husband Hur is suffocated by the spittle of the Jews*

In the last chapter we heard how Christ was betrayed; now let us consider how he is mocked, spit upon, and blindfolded. When the soldiers arrest and bind Christ, Peter cuts off the ear of one of the servants. Jesus immediately shows his mercy, touches the ear, and heals it instantly (John 18.10). They then lead Christ away to the house of Annas, the father-in-law of the high priest, Caiphas (John 18.13). When Annas interrogates him about his doctrine, Christ responds that he should question those who heard him. It was not his custom to speak in unfrequented places, but rather he spoke in the temple and in the synagogue where the people gathered (John 18.20). At this very instant, a servant of Annas washes his hands and then strikes Jesus on the face. This servant is believed to be Malchus whose ear Christ healed a short time previously. Christ neither defends himself nor strikes back, but humbly maintains his dignity with grace. Brethren, if any of you had received such a blow, and if you had the power Christ has, what would you have done? Perhaps, like Peter, you would have struck with a drawn sword, or like James and John you would have hurled upon them fire from the sky (Luke 9.54). We must not act in such a manner, brethren, but must attend to the teaching of Christ: If one will strike you on the cheek, offer him the other (Luke 6.29). The enemies of Christ lead him away, while he is bound, from the house of Annas,

and they lead him away with insults and injuries to the house of Caiphas (John 18.24). Here the elders gather to hold a council at which to find both occasion and cause to put Jesus to death. Every accusation they devised against him was either totally false or insufficient. So Caiphas then charged them to ask Christ, if he is the Son of the living God? Christ then swore that he is the Son of the living God. The council now concurs that because of this statement Christ should be put to death. They then cover his eyes with a cloth, defile his face with spittle, and strike him with their hands, inquiring what does he prophesy now, or who it might be who strikes him. Every insult they are able to devise, these enemies of Christ inflict upon him without mercy. These abuses, so scornful and wicked, lasted the entire night until morning in the house of Caiphas. O how great is the clemency and the patience of the Savior! O how great is the cruelty and folly of his enemies! The covered eyes of Christ see everything, and his enemies think that he who is omniscient does not know who strikes him. Angels delight to look upon this face that his enemies do not fear to defile with the most filthy spittle. The hands they dare to bind are indeed the hands that in the beginning fashioned heaven and earth.

Chapter 19

Figure 75. **Ham mocks his father, Noe, whereas the other brothers pity him**

Figure 76. **After having blinded Samson, the Philistines make a fool of him**

Mockingly and with gestures, they call him a prophet, he from whom the prophets of old received their power. They blind him with a cloth covering his eyes, he who deemed it worthy to illuminate their way with a pillar of fire (Exodus 13.21). They do not fear to cover his face with spittle, though he, a long time ago, marvelously covered them with a cloud. The idolaters of the molten calf prefigure those who strike his face with spittle. When the children of Israel wished to worship a foreign god, Aaron and Hur, husband of Miriam, opposed them. The Israelites became enraged, ran after Hur, and smothered him with spittle. They were angry with Hur because he opposed their idolatry just as the Pharisees are angry with Christ because he censured their teachings. Ham, son of Noe, prefigures the enemies of Christ who mock him with insults. Ham should have honored his father, but it is written that he wretchedly mocked and scorned him (Genesis 9.22–25). The enemies of Christ also should have shown him reverence, but they delight in scorning and dishonoring him. However much the son of Noe disgracefully insults his father, the mockery of Christ is much more degrading. Noe is derided in a tent where no one saw him, but Christ is insulted at the home of the high priest where a crowd is gathered. Noe is scorned while he was asleep and thus unaware,

but Christ is conscious and everyone sees and hears the insults. Only one son insults Noe, but the entire council derides and makes a fool of Christ. Noe's other two sons sympathized with their father, but Christ has no one to support him in any way whatsoever. The Philistines, enemies of Samson who blinded, captured, ridiculed and belittled him, prefigure all those who scorn Christ. Samson because of his great strength is a figure or type of Christ. Samson allowed himself to be bound once, and Christ also allows himself to be bound once. At another time it will please Samson to retaliate, and Christ, too, will wreak vengeance on his enemies at the end of the world when he comes in majesty and power. Neither Scripture nor any tongue is able to explain that Christ's enemies at that time will prefer to be sped to their punishment rather than to behold the enraged countenance of their judge and avenger. Then he will say, "Go you cursed into eternal fire" (Matthew 25.41), and to his friends, "Come you blessed and receive your eternal reward" (Matthew 25.34). O, good Jesus, give us the grace to serve you here peacefully that we may hear this blessed calling from you.

Chapter 20

Figure 77. *Jesus is tied to a column and scourged*

Figure 78. *Holofernes's servant ties Prince Achior to a tree*

In the last chapter we heard how Christ was jeered and blindfolded; and in the present chapter, let us hear how he is tied to a column. During the entire night his enemies subjected Christ to derision, and when the next morning came, they lead him to the Court of Justice of Pilate, the governor. When Pilate questions his accusers about the charges against Christ, they respond that he is a felon and a rabble rouser who misled all the people, not only those in Judea, but also those in his native land, Galilee. When Pilate heard that Christ was a Galilean, he remanded him to Herod because this matter pertains to his court. On this day Herod and Pilate, who were enemies, now became friends. Herod had never seen Christ, but had heard many things about him and is now very much pleased at his coming. Herod surmised that Christ is a learned man, a magician, or a necromancer, and he wants to see him perform some wondrous sign. Therefore, Herod questions Christ about many things, but Christ remains silent and does not respond in any way. Because of this behavior, Herod thought that Christ is mentally incompetent, so he makes sport of him, dressing him in a white garment. Next, Herod sends the prisoner back to Pilate's Court of Justice because he found no cause for the sentence of death (Luke 23.11). Herod was completely unaware of its significance when he clothed Christ in a white garment, for the Holy Spirit secretly caused this to show the innocence of Christ. Just as the Holy Spirit suggested through the mouth of Caiaphas the expediency of Christ's death,

he also demonstrates the innocence of Christ by the action of Herod. Pilate interrogates the enemies of Christ to see if they had a just cause strong enough to condemn him to death. They list three complaints against Jesus presenting them in this public tribunal before all: he said that he is able to destroy the temple of God made with hands, and after three days build another not made with hands (Mark 14.58). Also, he said that tribute should not be given to Caesar, Finally, he boasted that he is King of the Jews. Pilate judged the first two accusations to be frivolous, but he interrogated Christ carefully about the third charge. Caesar had brought the Kingdom of Judea under the control of imperial Rome, and the people of Judea at this time had no other king but Caesar. In fact Pilate himself was appointed governor of Judea by Caesar, and on this account he would not permit anyone to say that he is King of Judea. Jesus finally answered that his kingdom is not of this world. When Pilate heard this response, he then judged the third accusation to be worthless, too. But he wondered how he might appease the anger of the crowd, and so he decides to have Christ scourged. This expediency seemed to solve the problem of the crowd's contempt, and their petition for the death sentence. Now he would not have to render a decision of death on insufficient evidence. Pilate's soldiers then scourged Jesus, and bribed by the Pharisees, they gave him more lashes than were customary. Prince Achior whom the servants of Holofernes tied to a tree prefigures this flagellation.

Chapter 20

lamech gstrigit a mas sins weonbus
Job flagellabat a venone et ab vrore

Figure 79. **Lamech is held in check by his evil wives**

Figure 80. **Job is scourged by the devil and by his wife**

The attendants of Holofernes bind Achior to a tree, and Pilate's soldiers tie Christ to a column. Achior is bound because he spoke the truth, and Christ is scourged because he preached the truth. Achior is bound because he did not speak courteously to Holofernes, and Christ is restrained because he displeases and censures his enemies. Achior is bound because he praised the glory of God, and Christ is scourged because he makes known the name of the Father. Further, we must consider that Lamech's two wives, Sella and Ada, prefigure the people of two nations who scourge Christ. The two nations are the pagans and the people of the synagogue. Sella and Ada harassed their husband with words and beatings, and the pagans and the people of the synagogue scourge their Savior. The pagans beat him with whips and rods, and the people of the synagogue lash him with their tongues. These two flagellations that Christ suffers were prefigured a long time ago by holy Job. Job was whipped two ways. Satan scourged him with whips, and his wife lashed him with words, the one causing pain in his body, and the other causing pain in his heart. Satan felt the hurt that he caused in the flesh was not sufficient so that he instigated Job's wife to wound her husband's spirit. Likewise, it is not sufficient for the enemies of Christ to cut him to pieces with a whip,

Banderole: May the name of the Lord be blessed

but they must scourge him with the most cutting words. From the soles of his feet to the top of his head there was no soundness in Job, so too no part of his body is free from pain. As the body of Christ is more noble and delicate, so then much more severe and intense is his pain. Consider now how much suffering Christ endures for you, and do not again surrender your soul to perdition! Consider if you have ever seen or heard of such suffering as the Passion of Our Lord Jesus Christ! Consider how great is Christ's love for you and the anguish he endures! Now consider how much you have suffered for him, and how much gratitude and how much devotion you have given back to him! All the good works you do during the days of your life do not equal in value the smallest drop of his blood. Do not complain if you suffer a little in this life. Consider in your mind's eye the blood of Jesus Christ, and mix your bitterness with his blood so whatever you suffer will seem sweet to you. Suffer in this life a moderate flagellation so that you may flee eternal damnation in the future. Ask the Lord to chastise you in this life so that after death you may merit the Kingdom of Heaven without any punishment. O, good Jesus, strike us with a scourge now so that we may taste the heavenly honey without purgatory.

Chapter 21

Cultus conatur spinea corona

donibia ihus coun ihr aacptm libnpi ipo sint

Figure 81. **Christ is crowned with thorns**

Figure 82. **The concubine takes the king's crown and crowns herself**

In the last chapter we heard how Christ was scourged; now let us consider how he is crowned with thorns. Pilate orders his soldiers to scourge Jesus, but Christ's enemies bribe the guards to apply more lashes than is customary. According to the law, no more than 40 stripes are to be given (Deuteronomy 25.3), but his enemies wish the number to be increased. They even felt the increased number of lashes is not sufficient so they contrive a new punishment, the crowning with thorns. They now honor him as a king, vest him in a purple garment, and put a royal insignia, a scepter, in his hand. It was customary at that time to scourge a criminal once, and it was not lawful to crown a person with thorns. O wicked enemies of Christ, inventors of a new form of torture, how many new punishments will you invent! These inventors of new devices of torture shall themselves suffer new and unheard of torments! The measure they shall measure with shall be measured to them (Luke 6.38), and many new torments shall be added, for the pain never ceases. After they scourged Jesus, they do not clothe him, but rather vest him in a purple cloak. Since the color purple is a royal insignia, they disguise Christ as a king to make a fool of him. The second royal insignia is the crown of gold and in its place they crown him with thorns. The third royal insignia is the golden scepter,

and in its place they put a reed in his right hand. A subject ordinarily genuflects to honor his king, and this is the way they salute Christ. It is customary to offer gifts to a king and following this custom they slap and spit upon him and repeatedly strike him upon the head with a rod in order to press the crown of thorns even deeper and to cause a sharper sting. O impious enemies of Christ, why do you treat your king so cruelly, and why do you not recognize the kindness he has shown you? In Arnon he planted a sharp rock under your feet (Numbers 21.13–15), but your cruelty pierced his head with sharp thorns. He showed pity to your shoes and your feet (Deuteronomy 29.5), and you show irreverence to his head. He preserved your garments from corruption for 40 years, but you strip him of his clothing mockingly. On your account he scourged the Pharao and Egypt (Exodus 7–14), but you scourged him without cause. Again on your account he, through Moses, broke the crown of the King of Egypt, but you place a crown of thorns on his head. He brought low all the kings of the earth before you, but you are thankless and pay homage to him as a king, mockingly. He honored you above all the nations, but you dishonored him with all your senseless games. He alone miraculously overcame your enemies, one pursuing 1,000 (Isaias 30.17), and, earlier, 10,000 fleeing from two (Leviticus 26.8), but you gather against Christ who stands alone and you unite two nations against one man.

Chapter 21

Figure 83. *Semei curses David*

Figure 84. **King Hanon dishonors David's messengers**

One pursues 1,000, and 10,000 flee from two by the will of God, and for a reason it comes to pass. How did all of you seize Christ unless God delivered him to you? The jeering of Christ in this coronation was prefigured a long time ago by a concubine of the king [Darius] (1 Esdras 4.29 also known in the Vulgate as 3 Esdras). The concubine seized the crown from the head of the king and puts it on her own head. Likewise, the enemies of Christ stole his crown, the honor due to him, and then with a crown of thorns disgraced him. The concubine slapped the king on the face with the palm of her hand, and the king endured this insult without becoming indignant. In the same manner, the King of Heaven endures the slaps and punches of his enemies and does not show any outrage. The king loved his concubine and patiently tolerates everything she does as a jest, just as Christ proves that he loves his enemies by patiently suffering these humiliations. King David prefigures the patience of Christ when he meekly endured so much mischief from the vicious Semei (2 Kings 16.5–10). Semei threw sticks, stones and mud at David just as the enemies of Christ slap and spit upon him; Semei called David a murderer and a son of Belial just as Christ's persecutors call him a seducer of the people and a criminal.

Abisai would have killed Semei, but David did not permit it, just as the angels would have killed those mocking Christ, but he did not allow it. Christ came into this world not to kill anyone but rather to die for our sins and to reconcile us to the Father, to restore peace and concord and to build a bridge between God and man. Christ's enemies did not treat him as a peacemaker but insulted him with their cruel jests. On this account, the messengers of King David prefigure Christ since Hanon, King of the Ammonites, disgraced the couriers shamefully (2 Kings 10.1–5). David sent these emissaries to offer peace, but King Hanon cut away their garments up to their buttocks and shaved off half their beards. Likewise the Son of God resolved to establish peace in this world, but his enemies strip him of his garments and soil his beard with spittle. Christ indeed came to restore a peace between God and man that only he was able to establish after 5,000 years. The heathens spill blood when they establish peace, and the Jews customarily perform a libation of water (Hebrews 9.19), but Christ shed both blood and water so that we may more steadfastly keep the peace he establishes. The pagans pour the blood of animals in their libation, and the Jews pour the water of the river in their ceremony, but Christ shed his own blood and water from his side. O, good Jesus, teach us to preserve this tranquillity so that we may merit dwelling with you in eternal peace.

Chapter 22

Figure 85. **Christ carries his cross**

Figure 86. **Isaac carries the wood for his sacrifice**

In the last chapter we heard how Christ is crowned with thorns; now let us consider how he bears his cross. After Christ was scourged, made a fool of, and crowned with thorns, Pilate presents him to the people to show them how he had been treated (John 19.2–6). He acted accordingly, thinking that the people would be satisfied with the ill treatment and bodily pain Christ suffered, and therefore they would be content and cease to ask for his death. However, the mob gnashing their teeth, and raging as mad dogs shouted in reply, "Crucify, crucify him." Eager to free Christ, Pilate announced that he wished to set free one of the prisoners. But the angry mob insists that he free the thief, Barabbas, and demands that Christ be handed over to be crucified. O cruel enemies of Christ! Why do you not petition that he be set free, he who delivered you from the captivity of Babylon and Egypt? Pilate seeing that he could not prevail and that the mob is becoming riotous, washes his hands to show he is innocent of the blood of Jesus. The Holy Spirit secretly influenced Pilate to act accordingly, signaling that Jesus, both innocent and just, would die. Pilate's wife claims she had seen in a dream many things about Jesus, and he must be set free for he is a just man. All this attempted delay is caused by the devil eager to halt the progress of the Passion and put an end to our redemption. Because Pilate only now at this late hour presses for the freedom of Christ, many think he too acted

at the instigation of the devil. The devil thus manipulates Pilate and his wife to terminate our redemption just as he initiated our damnation a long time ago through Adam and Eve. For when the devil sees the holy fathers of old rejoicing in limbo, he concludes that Christ wishes to set them free through his Passion. Therefore, he presses on to stop the suffering of Christ, trying to manipulate Pilate by the influence of his wife. O the beguiling snare of the devil is the flattering woman whose charm leads man to his ruin! Pilate's soldiers now strip Christ of his purple robe and return his own garment. Next they place upon his shoulder the cross he must bear, and this is indeed Christ's supreme indignity. At this time a cross was a cursed thing, and neither the soldiers nor the enemies of Christ wished to carry it. Now the cursed and contemptible cross has become blessed and glorious by the Passion of Christ and what was then the cross of thieves and the punishment of robbers is now traced upon the forehead of princes, kings, and emperors. At that time vicious criminals, comrades of the devil, were suspended from the beams of the cross, but now the devil is punished by it and flees from the presence of a cross. In a former age Isaac, the son of Abraham, prefigured Jesus Christ bearing his cross. Isaac bore on his little shoulders the wood his father intended to use to sacrifice him to the Lord (Genesis 22.6). Likewise Christ bears on his shoulders a cross from which his enemies wish to suspend him.

Chapter 22

Figure 87. **The heir of the vineyard is cast out and killed***

Figure 88. **The spies carry a cluster of grapes on a pole***

Isaac aided by an angel is set free and a ram caught in a bramble is sacrificed in his place. Neither a ram nor any other creature suffers in place for Christ, but he alone bears all and is sacrificed for us. When Isaac heard that his father wished to offer him to the Lord, he responded that he freely wishes to be sacrificed. In the same manner the Son of God obeys his heavenly Father even unto death and offers himself freely to his every command. The Father, Son, and the Holy Spirit had a secret meeting to make a plan to send one of their number to save the human race. When the Father said, "Whom will I send, and who will go?" the Son answers, "Send me for I am now ready!" "Go," replies the Father, "into the world and dwell among men, bearing patiently whatever they do to you." Therefore the Son of the living God is sent and dwells in Judea, but they did not receive him, for he is brutally killed. While he was preaching, Christ intimated in a parable that this would happen, using the figure of a vineyard. A certain man planted a vineyard, built a wall around it, constructed a tower and a press within the wall, and then entrusted it to his tenants. At the time of the harvest, the owner of the vineyard sent his servants to collect his profits. The tenants captured the servants, beat some of them and murdered the others. When this was reported to the lord of the vineyard, he sent more men than before, but they suffered the same fate as the previous group. Finally, the lord sent his only son

whom the tenants apprehended, cast out of the vineyard, and tortured to death more savagely than they treated the servants. The vineyard in the parable signifies Judea and the people of Judea; the enclosed wall represents Jerusalem; the tower is a figure for the temple of Solomon, and the wine press stands for the altar of burnt offerings and sacrificial oblations. The servants who were sent represent the prophets who were tortured and killed in diverse ways. Isaias was sawed in half, Jeremias was stoned, Ezechiel was made mad, and Amos was perforated by nails. Finally, the Heavenly Father sends his only Son, Jesus Christ, and he is treated more savagely than the others. They placed a cross upon his shoulders and remove him from his vineyard, Jerusalem, and finally put him to death. The two people who put him to death are the Jews and the gentiles, the Jews in their hearts and the gentiles in their deeds. The two explorers who carry the grapes from the promised land to the desert prefigure both the Jews and the gentiles. Jesus Christ, the Son of God, is the cluster of grapes carried by these two people from Jerusalem to Calvary. The Israelites are able to judge the bounty of the promised land by the grapes, and we are able to consider the bounty of heaven by the teachings of Christ. O, good Jesus, teach us to consider the sweetness of eternal life so that we may dwell with you for all eternity.

* The captions for blocks 87 and 88 have been reversed by the carver.

Chapter 23

Figure 89. **The crucified Christ predicts his death**

Figure 90. **The inventors of the arts of working with metals and making melodies**

In the last chapter we heard how Christ bore his cross; now we shall learn how he prays for his tormentors. Because of the abuse he suffered throughout the day and night, he is so weakened that it became evident that he is not strong enough to carry his cross. They therefore compel Simon of Cyrene to help Jesus bear the cross (Matthew 27.32). When he arrives at Calvary, they observe that he is so fatigued that they give him vinegar with gall mixed with wine and myrrh. The malicious enemies of Christ made this drink as foretold by the prophetic Psalmist (Matthew 27.34; Psalms 68.22). The soldiers then take the cross from Jesus, place it on the ground, strip Christ of his garments, and extend him upon the cross. They fasten the right hand to the cross with a nail, then stretching the other hand with a rope to align it with a hole in the beam. After the left hand is fastened to the cross, the legs are extended with the aid of a rope and fastened to the cross with one nail. The Lord spoke about this crucifixion in the Psalms saying, "They have dug my hands and feet and they have numbered all my bones" (Psalms 21.17–18). After Jesus suffered this most cruel torture, he showed his tormentors his most merciful charity. He prays to his Heavenly Father for them, and gives us an example for loving our enemies. Indeed, when we love our enemies and pray for them, we show that we are sons of God and brothers of Christ. Christ teaches us to love our enemies,

so that we may become Sons of his Father who dwells in heaven. To love one's benefactors and friends is normal and ordinary, but to love one's persecutors and enemies is indeed extraordinary. The soldiers secure Christ to the cross on the ground and then raise it aloft. The prayer Christ offers was prefigured by Jubal and Tubalcain, sons of Lamech, who are recognized as the inventors of iron making and music. When Tubalcain struck the hammer, Jubal invented music from the sound of the hammer striking the iron. To such a melody, the sound of the pounding of iron, we can compare the prayer of Christ from the cross. When his torturers fastened him to the cross, Christ chanted to his Father a most pleasing melody, "Father forgive them, for they know not what they do, for they do not recognize me to be your Son." Indeed, if the Jews and Romans had recognized the Son of God, they would never have crucified the King of Glory. This blessed melody was so pleasant and pleasing that 3,000 were converted at that same hour. Well were the enemies of Christ prefigured by the first iron makers, for these same enemies invented a new manner of crucifixion. It was not lawful to fasten a man to the cross with nails, but rather he was to be held in place by ropes and suspended on the cross until death.

Chapter 23

Figure 91. **Isaias the prophet is cut in half by a saw**

Figure 92. **King Moab sacrifices his son on the wall**

Truly the inventors of music prefigured Christ because he is the first to sing such a melody to God. Christ not only prays for those who crucified him, but urgently petitions the Father for the salvation of everyone. Although many have prayed in the past for the sins of humankind, no prayers or sacrifices were as efficacious as those of Christ who prayed with tears and such urgency. His prayer is heard and respectfully granted. Isaias who was put to death most inhumanely prefigures the crucifixion of Christ. Isaias's enemies cut him in two and in so doing fitly foreshadow the death of Christ insofar as the enemies of Christ divide him in two, separating his soul from his body by means of the cross. Although they separate the body from the soul, never do they have the power to separate the deity from one or the other. The deity does not depart from his body at death, nor does it likewise leave the soul in any fashion whatsoever. God does not wish to abandon his Son; he wishes only to save humankind. O what inestimable love our heavenly Father shows us to offer his beloved son in sacrifice for us! O the magnitude of the divine charity to sacrifice his beloved Son for our sins! Who has ever seen or has ever heard of such love?

Who is able to explain this love in full? At an earlier time King Moab prefigures the immense love of the Father. The king's enemies surround the city, and the citizens within lack food and drink and grow weak. The king loved his subjects so much that he sacrifices his son for them. The besieged city prefigures the world, and the citizens designate the human race. The city is so completely blockaded by a legion of demons, and all the inhabitants are so weakened that they do not have the strength to overcome the siege. Finally, the Father of Mercy and the God of Consolation looks upon our plight, and so loves us that he sacrifices his Son to free us from the snares of the devil. King Moab suffers his son to die for the king's friends and subjects, but God offers his Son for his enemies. With what can we repay so great a love? We can repay this love only if we become zealous and love him wholeheartedly. We love him because he loved us first and looked upon our captivity with great concern. O, good Jesus, grant that we may love you in this world so that we may dwell with you in the future world.

Chapter 24

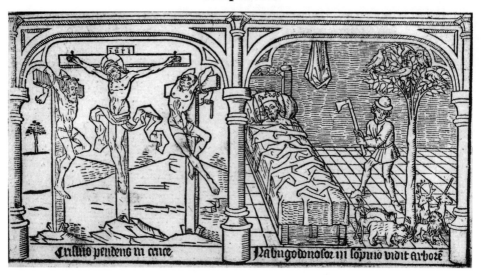

*Figure 93. **Christ hangs from the cross***

*Figure 94. **In a dream Nabuchodonosor sees a tree***

In the last chapter we heard how Christ prayed on the cross for his tormentors; now let us hear how his death is prefigured. King Nabuchodonosor saw in a dream a large tree, which grew to the highest heaven and whose branches spread throughout the world (Daniel 4). The literal meaning of the dream signifies the power of King Nabuchodonosor, but the mystical meaning prefigures Christ the King of the world to come, whose power rises above all earthly might up to heaven and is spread throughout the world. All the beasts of the earth and birds of the air dwell within this power and are fed and nourished from all its fruits. This analogy aptly shows that every creature is sustained through the grace of Christ. But an angel shall come and order the tree to be cut down, prefiguring the crucifixion of Christ. The angel also says that all the branches are to be cut from the tree to suggest that all the disciples are separated from Christ. The angel adds that all the leaves are to be shaken from the tree to indicate that all the teachings of Christ are held in contempt by his enemies, and that all the fruits of the tree are to be scattered to indicate that the works of Christ are held for naught by his enemies. The angel says further that the beasts and the birds should flee from the tree because neither men nor angels may offer help for Christ. The angel says that although the tree is to be cut down, its roots must be permitted to regenerate, indicating that although Christ is about to die

his death shall not be permanent — he will rise again. The angel then tells Nabuchodonosor the literal meaning of the tree, saying that it should be bound in iron and brass bands to show that Christ is bound to a column and fastened to the cross with iron nails. The angel also says that Nabuchodonosor ought to be moistened with dew from heaven meaning literally that he would die alone and prefigure that Christ would be crucified outside the city and likewise be moistened with a heavenly dew — that is, bathed in his own blood. The angel says that this same king must be fed as the beasts are fed, indicating that Christ must drink gall and vinegar. The angel adds that the king's heart ought to be changed from a human heart to the heart of a beast because the enemies of Jesus do not treat him as a human being but rather as a wild beast or a worm that they spit upon and crucify. The enemies of Christ do not act as human beings toward Jesus but hiss and make animal sounds at him. The angel also says the span of the King's life should extend over seven periods of time because the Passion of Christ extends through the seven canonical hours. The angel concludes that this is the interpretation, the secret of the dream according to the judgment of the angels and the interpretation of the saints. All this indicates that the death of Christ is necessary for both the angels and the saints because through Christ the restoration of the angels and the liberation of the saints are completed. The angel says this king should be known to all because God on high rules over all the

Chapter 24

Figure 95. **King Codrus gives his life for his subjects**

Figure 96. **After Eleazar stabs the elephant, he is crushed by it**

kingdoms of men, and by the preaching of Christ and his followers the world is shown the true God of all the ages. The angel says that God may give a kingdom to whomever He wishes, and He ordinarily appoints the most humble to rule over men. Because Christ is the most humble, God therefore establishes him to be the King of all men. Now it is evident how this tree prefigures Christ who is crucified for us by the decree of the Father. The Heavenly Father preordains the Passion of Christ, and the Son accepts it not unwillingly but freely indeed. Codrus, a king of ancient Greece, prefigures this free choice because he accepted death willingly to free his subjects. The city of Athens was under siege, and no one was coming to liberate it. The king took counsel with the god Apollo to see if there were any way to save the city. Although the king was a pagan and did not know the true God, he nevertheless received the correct response from Apollo by God's permission. The king learns that it is impossible to save the city unless the enemy kill him. The king so loved his subjects that he goes forth to die for them. However, when the enemy discover the king's plan, they are unwilling to kill him. When the king learns of their view, he returns to the city,

changes his royal attire for servant's garb and goes forth again from the city. Immediately the enemy rush toward him and kill him, not having recognized the king dressed as a servant. When they finally identify the dead king, they give up their assault of the city, cease their attack, and return to their homeland. Christ loves us in the same way. He dies for us willingly and frees us from the bondage of the devil. He clothes himself with a human body, the garment of a servant, because no one is able to kill him in the regal attire of his deity. If they had recognized him to be the King of Glory, never would anyone have killed him. Not only did Christ break the bondage of our captivity, but by his death he slew death. Eleazar, the Machabean, prefigures this fact a long time ago when he exposed himself to death to destroy an elephant clad in an armor breastplate. When the army attacked the Israelites, Eleazar ran toward the elephant to pierce it with a lance, and the mortally wounded animal fell upon its slayer and crushed him. The strong fought the mighty and both fell in ruin; both Eleazar and the elephant are killed. So Christ the strong assailed mighty death, and by his death he slew our death. O, good Jesus, who liberates us by your death, grant us that we may live forever after this life.

Chapter 25

Figure 97. **Mary's sorrow for her Son**

Figure 98. **Jacob laments for his son Joseph**

In the last chapter we considered the death of our Lord Jesus Christ; now let us hear the sorrows of his most sweet mother. When our Savior suffered the Passion, Mary was in seclusion but bore with her son all his pain, compassionately fulfilling the words spoken by Simeon the Just, "A sword shall pierce your soul" (Luke 2.35). Jacob's lament for his son Joseph (Genesis 37) prefigures the grief Mary bears for her son. Jacob loved Joseph more than his other sons; therefore, the envious sons plot to kill their brother. Jacob makes an embroidered damask tunic in various colors with scenes skillfully executed for Joseph and then sends him to his brothers where they were keeping their sheep. Upon arrival they seize him and wish to put him to death, but Joseph is protected by God and, instead, his brothers sell him to the Ismaelites. The brothers rend apart Joseph's tunic, sprinkle it with the blood of a goat, and send it with a messenger to their father to determine whether it is their brother's tunic. When Jacob sees it, he rends his own garments and begins to bewail that his son was surely devoured by a wild beast. His sons, hearing their father, offer their condolence to comfort him in his grief. But Jacob persists in his grief and tells them that he did not want any condolences, but he would descend into the lower regions to lament his son

for he does not wish to be comforted in this life. Mary likewise so sorrowed for her son that she would have descended into limbo to be with him if it were possible. Most dear brethren, how much do you think Mary laments when she sees his garment, his lacerated flesh? Joseph's tunic is moistened with the blood of a goat, but the garment of Christ, his body, is soaked in his own blood; and wild beasts, his most envious enemies, attack Christ. Jacob rends his garments because of his grief, but Mary rends the garment of her interior powers. All the sons of Jacob gather around their father, but they are unable to lessen his sorrow. If the whole world gathered around Mary, she, without her son, would never be consoled. Jacob laments the loss of one although he still has 12 sons, but how much greater is Mary's grief since she lost her only son. The sorrow of Mary is also precisely prefigured when Cain murdered Abel. Adam and Eve grievously lamented Abel's death; in fact, they mourned his loss for over 100 years. But however great their sorrow appears to be, it pales in comparison with Mary's pain because the more intense one loves, deeper is the grief at the loss of the loved one.

Chapter 25

Figure 99. **The first parents mourn the death of Abel**

Figure 100. **Noemi bewails the death of her sons**

Never was there a greater love than the love between Mary and her son; therefore, we shall never find a sorrow equal to Mary's grief. Adam and Eve grieved for a long time, in fact 100 years, but if Christ had been dead 100,000 years, Mary would never have ceased grieving. When Joseph took the body of Christ down from the cross, Mary is present to take the body into her arms. There was a little packet of myrrh between her breasts just as it is sung about in the Canticle of Canticles (1.12). O how bitter is the packet of myrrh in Mary's heart, bearing all the pain that Christ suffered for a night and a day! As much as wine is proven to be sweet and noble, it is bitter and sharp when it has turned sour. Likewise, as much as Mary's love is sweet and noble, then the more bitter is her sorrow during the Passion. Noemi, who lamented her two sons, prefigures Mary (Ruth 1.1–22). Noemi said, "Do not call me Noemi," for the name means beautiful, but rather she said, "Call me Mara," meaning bitter. "O why has the almighty filled me with such bitterness," she said while weeping for her children's death. Noemi foreshadows Mary, who mourns not for one son but two. One son is by natural birth, but the other son mother Mary cares for by adoption. Of course, Jesus is her true and natural son, and the adopted son is the entire human race. The natural son died in body, but the adopted son has died in spirit. Mary suffers the most bitter sorrow for both her sons because she loves them deeply. Although Mary loves her natural son more than she loves herself, she nevertheless suffers him to die to free us. Our most sweet mother prefers Jesus to be tortured so that we are not condemned to perpetual death. From this example we are able to weigh how much Mary loves us, for she wishes her own beloved son to die for our salvation. When presents are exchanged, the one received seems to be appreciated more than the one given. It appears Mary loves us more than she loved her own son because she wants him to be crucified so we are not damned. Also from this example we know how much the Heavenly Father loves us since he gives his Son to die for us. Therefore, both the Father and the Mother love us immensely, and they rightly deserve to be loved by us completely. O, good Jesus, give us this love so we may merit dwelling in heaven with you for all eternity.

Chapter 26

Figure 101. *At Compline Jesus is buried*

Figure 102. *David weeps at the funeral for Abner*

In the last chapter we heard how Christ is taken down from the cross; now let us hear how he is buried. Joseph and Nicodemus wrap his body in a linen cloth, anoint it with aromatic spices, and place it in the sepulcher. Mary stands by, sighing and lamenting and pouring forth tears. Words cannot describe her pain, nor can anyone appreciate the depth of her sorrow. She is exhausted beyond measure because of the ordeal during this long night and day, and with extreme difficulty she follows the funeral procession of her Son to the sepulcher. She draws his body close with embraces and kisses, and all good people pity her, defend her and say, "O that such cruelty of such wicked men is used against a woman so meek and mild!" This lady makes such an extraordinary lamentation that those standing by are moved to compassion and tears. Who does not pity such a troubled mother? Who does not grieve because of such sorrow and tears? Now she kisses the hands and feet of her Son; now she embraces his neck and touches his side. Now she repeatedly strikes her breast with her fist; now she wrings her hands and weeps profusely. Now she looks upon the wounds of her Son, now the eyes; now she falls to the ground and kisses his chest and his mouth. One would have the heart of a beast not to be moved to compassion by such tears and agony. Even an animal is moved by another's crying, and who now does not pity this most troubled mother? Jesus was compassionate and wept with Mary Magdalene, and now who does not weep and mourn with the Virgin? It is said that dolphins mourn and bury their dead; how then can one hear the complaints of Mary and not grieve with her? The sorrow that Mary bears at the burial of Christ was prefigured a long time ago at the funeral of Abner. Joab deceitfully murders Abner, and King David laments as he followed the funeral procession. Not only did David weep at the funeral, but his example was the occasion for others to weep. "Rend your garments," he said, "and weep. Do you know that the greatest prince in Israel fell today?" (2 Kings 3.38). Jesus was not killed as an unknown nor as a criminal but as a just and honorable person. So the Blessed Virgin may have said on that Good Friday when her Son was put to death by his enemies, "Rend your garments, your interior spirit, and mourn with me!" "Are you aware that the greatest prince of Israel is slain on this day for whom every creature shows sympathy?" The sun withdraws its ray so that Christ is not burned, and the day becomes dark so his nakedness is not seen.

Chapter 26

*Figure 103. **Joseph is cast into the well***   *Figure 104. **A whale devours Jonas***

The earth trembles to frighten his tormentors; the veil of the temple is split; and the Pharisees lament. Boulders break in two, and with their deafening noise cry out to break the silence of the disciples. The graves break open, and the dead walk forth to show the power of the prince of the world. The devil sitting at the left side of the cross wonders who it might be that everyone honors. The Athenian Philosophers, as the sun darkens, proclaim that the god of nature is in a perilous condition, and so they build an altar to an unknown god who will be known sometime in the future. We deeply mourn at the funeral of this prince and our hearts are broken with grief! The sons of Jacob who cast their brother, Joseph, into a cistern prefigure by their action the burial of Christ. They hated their brother so much that they would kill him without cause just as the enemies of Christ despised their brother. The sons of Jacob sold their brother for 30 denarii, just as Judas sold Christ to his enemies for the same price. The sons of Jacob tear Joseph's tunic in two, and the enemies of Christ wound his flesh with rods, whips, thorns, and nails. Joseph's tunic did not sense any pain or sorrow,

but Christ suffers his Passion throughout his entire body. Joseph's tunic covered his entire body, but in the body of Christ there is no wholeness to be found from his head to the soles of his feet. Jacob's sons sprinkle the blood of a goat on Joseph's garment, but the enemies of Christ dye his body with his own blood. The sons of Jacob trouble their father excessively, but the enemies of Christ inflict upon his mother, Mary, the greatest sorrow possible. Joseph forgave his brothers for what they did to him, but Christ prays to his Father for his tormentors. Joseph, sold by his brothers, becomes Lord of Egypt, but Christ, crucified by his enemies, becomes Lord of heaven and earth. Later, the sons of Jacob honor their brother, and after his Resurrection, many believe in Christ. When Jacob heard that his son is alive, he rejoices, and when Mary saw that Christ rose from the dead, she is most happy. Joseph grows to be a prosperous and successful son, and the faith of Christ, Christianity, spreads throughout the world day by day. Finally, Jonas who was thrown from a boat into the sea and swallowed by a whale also prefigures the burial of Christ. Jonas was in the whale for three days and three nights just as Christ was in the sepulcher for three days. However, how this story relates to Christ is made clear in the chapter on the Resurrection. O, good Jesus, may we so honor your burial that we may merit not to be separated from you!

Chapter 27

Figure 105. **The holy fathers are freed from the lower world**

Figure 106. **Israel's liberation from the Pharao**

In the last chapter we heard how Christ is buried; let us now hear how he frees the holy fathers from prison. After Christ died on the cross on Good Friday, his soul, always united to the deity, immediately enters the lower regions not as some think to await Sunday, but rather to hasten there to console the imprisoned. If anyone were able to free a friend, it would be a crime to wait for three days. Therefore, Christ our most faithful friend does not tarry, but immediately after his Passion he visits the holy ones in their prison. By his haste Christ gives us an example of how to help the poor souls, and not to tarry and prolong their suffering. This is most serious, for one who suffers indescribable pain is not tested further with delay. Some have 30 Masses, extended over a period of 30 days, said for their dear one. This is indeed good, but it is much better for the poor soul to have all the Masses celebrated on the first day. It is painful for the poor soul to wait for 30 days. This applies to all the suffering souls. Therefore, hasten quickly to aid the souls in purgatory and follow the example of Christ. Christ does not free the holy fathers immediately, but remains with them so they may enjoy his sweet presence. In the middle of the night before he arose from the dead, he then leads them forth from the captivity of the devil. This diabolical captivity

is prefigured in a former age by the Egyptian captivity. The children of Israel were gravely oppressed by the Pharao of Egypt, and they cried out to the Lord for their freedom. The merciful Lord appears to Moses in the burning bush, which though completely ignited, remains green and whole. The Lord then sends Moses to the Pharao to free the children of Israel. Likewise, the prince of darkness imprisons the entire human race that repeatedly cries out to the Lord for redemption: "O God come to my assistance!" (Psalm 69.1); "Deliver me because I am poor and needy, for I have nothing by which I may free myself!" (Psalm 108.21); "Put forth your hand to deliver me!" (Psalm 143.7); "Send forth your lamb, a victim of reconciliation for you!" (Isaias 16.1); "Send forth your light to remove the darkness from me!" (Psalm 42.3); "Send forth your truth that your prophets be found faithful!" (Ecclesiasticus 36.18). Man cries out to the Lord for salvation by the holy prophets and in many other different ways. The merciful Lord frees man in the following manner: he descends into a burning bush that burns but remains whole. That is, the Lord descends into The Virgin Mary who remains a virgin. The Lord strikes the Pharao and all his people and leads the Israelites into a land flowing with milk and honey. So Christ likewise strikes the devil and all his crew, and he leads the saints of the Old Law to the eternal banquet.

Chapter 27

Ilirratio Abraha de ur calteoni.   Iiberatio lotþ a fodomis

*Figure 107. **The liberation of Abraham from Ur of the Chaldees***

*Figure 108. **The liberation of Lot from Sodom***

There they are fed milk, the sweet appearance of Christ's humanity, and honey, the sweet flowing contemplation of his divinity. When the Lord wished to liberate the Jews, he orders a lamb to be sacrificed (Exodus 12.3–11); when he willed to liberate us, he sacrifices himself. God prefigures this liberation of man when he frees Abraham from Ur of the Chaldees. Ur means fire and the people of the Chaldees worship fire as a god, and when Abraham would not worship the fire, they cast him into it. The true God whom Abraham cherished and worshiped mercifully frees him from the Chaldean fire. Just as God protected Abraham from burning within the fire, so too He protects the holy fathers from pain within limbo. Just as God rescued Abraham and made him the father of many nations, so He frees the holy fathers from the lower regions and joins them to the assembly of angels. God prefigures this redemption of man when He frees Lot from the destruction of Sodom. Only the good are freed from Sodom, and all the wicked perish in the fire and sulphur; so Christ only redeems the good from limbo, and he does not rescue any of the damned from hell. Therefore no one may say that God destroys hell, and who is able to repair it? Hell is not destroyed, and whoever enters there from the beginning of the world shall never be rescued but will always remain there. O, God, deem it worthy to protect us from that infernal region,

to punish us mercifully and purify us in this life! You inflict us here with tortures, scourges, and plagues so that you may deliver us from everlasting suffering! Whomever you love, you will castigate here; therefore, we beseech you most just God that you will so love us. It is better for us to come to you after we have suffered adversities than to enter eternal life after we have enjoyed temporal prosperity. You are aware that we are not tolerant of penance, but you intend to save us through penance whether we are willing or not. We are weak, and unable to bear up without complaint, but you, most just Lord, forgive us our impatience. The Lord ordered Lot and his wife to ascend a mountain and not to look back, but to turn their attention to the climb. So we, likewise, whom God frees from sin through penance ought not look back to the enjoyment of the sins we have left, but rather we should ascend higher from virtue to virtue and accomplish meritorious works of satisfaction. Lot's wife looks back and is turned to stone, and wild animals of the desert and other beasts lick this same stone. We likewise are hardened to stone by our relapses and are grasped and licked by the infernal beast. Therefore, let us ascend the mountain of virtue to be saved, and let us not look back lest we suffer damnation by our relapse. O, good Jesus, teach us to ascend and to love heaven so that we may merit to dwell with you in your holy mountain.

Chapter 28

Resurrectio dñi nri ihu xpi   Sampson tulit portas gaze

Figure 109. **The Resurrection of our Lord Jesus Christ**

Figure 110. **Samson carries off the gates of Gaza**

In the last chapter we heard about Christ's descent into Limbo; now let us hear about his glorious Resurrection. It is known that the Lord's sepulcher was carved out of a rock and consisted of two rooms. On entering the first chamber, one sees the second room with a connecting wall and a floor above the ground. The rock is seven or eight feet in length and its width is about the same; its height is as far as one is able to extend his hand. From the first chamber, one enters the second room through a small door that has about the same measurements as the first room. Entering the second chamber through the small door and looking to the right, one sees where the body was placed on a bench that extends from wall to wall and is about three feet wide. The height of the bench is about a foot and a half, and is not hollowed out; therefore, the body is placed atop it. Some pilgrims have called this bench the sepulcher, but the Jews call the entire rock with the two chambers the sepulcher. The doorway of the tomb is closed with a heavy stone and secured by the seal of the Jewish community in such a way that the body is not stolen. Further, they turned their attention to watchmen, pagan mercenaries, whom they stationed to guard the sepulcher. However, Christ passes through the closed door and the secure seal

because of the power of his glorified body. Next, an angel of the Lord comes down from heaven in the form of a man and rolls back the stone from the door as the guards look on. The face of the angel is exceedingly radiant and his garment is white. The earth trembles and the terrified guards fall to the earth as though they are dead. When the guards recover, they return to the Jews and report everything in the order that it happened. After a meeting, the Jews gave the guards a large sum of money to spread a false rumor about Christ, and to say that while they were sleeping the body was stolen. This is the story that the guards reported everywhere. Next we must consider how Samson and his great strength prefigure the glorious Resurrection of Christ. Samson enters the city of his enemies (Judges 16.1–3), and staying for the night, he sleeps there. His foes, however, lock the gates of the city, and they plot to kill him in the morning. Samson arises from his sleep in the middle of the night, and carries off the gates of the city with their posts. Christ, the strong one, likewise enters the city of his enemy, limbo, and remains there until the vigil of Sunday. In the middle of the night after causing havoc in limbo, Christ's soul unites to his body, and he who was dead now rises from the dead. Many bodies of the saints rose with him, and they enter the city of Jerusalem, appearing to many people.

Chapter 28

Figure 111. **The emergence of Jonas from the whale's stomach**

Figure 112. **The rejected block is made the cornerstone**

We do not expect that the bodies rose up on the eve of the Sabbath, but on that day the tombs are opened. Christ, the first born of the dead, rose first and then the bodies of the saints arose after him. Later they ascended with him, and we must not believe that they were to die again. Jonas, who remained alive for three days in the belly of the whale, prefigures the Resurrection of Christ. Jonas was aboard a vessel, tossed about by a storm at sea, and all were in peril of death. Jonas tells his mates to cast him overboard to lessen the fury of the sea and its danger. When they toss him into the sea, a whale immediately swallows him, and three days later it cast him up upon the shore. The treacherous sea represents the world, and in this world we are exposed to the dangers of the loss of eternal life. Christ freely gives himself up to death upon the cross to free us from this everlasting danger. God preserves Christ's body uncorrupted, and on the third day he raises him from the dead. A block of stone the builders rejected also prefigures the Resurrection of our Savior. During the time of Solomon when the Temple of the Lord was being constructed, someone found an extraordinary block of stone. The masons were unable to find a suitable place for it,

and many workers tried repeatedly. The stone block is either much too long or too thick, either much too short or too narrow. Therefore the angry masons reject it, and everyone calls it the rejected block. When the construction of the temple was completed, a cornerstone had to be set in place to join the two walls and complete the work. No stone could be found to fit the space to enable the masons to lay the foundation. Finally, they try the stone block that had been rejected and discovered that it fits best as the cornerstone. Everyone is amazed at such a wondrous event, and some added that a great future happening is foretold by this event. Christ is this rejected stone in his Passion, and he is made the cornerstone of the Church by his Resurrection. This fulfills the great prophecy, "The stone which the builders rejected, the same is become the head of the corner. This is the lord's doing and it is wonderful in our eyes" (Psalms 117.22–23). This prophecy is sung on the Feast of the Resurrection. As the cornerstone connects the two walls of the temple, so Christ builds one church of two nations, the gentiles and the Jews, cemented together in this building with his blood and joined with his most sacred body, the cornerstone. O, good Jesus, grant that we may so live in the church that we may merit to be with you for eternity in your heavenly temple.

Chapter 29

*Figure 113. **The Last Judgment***

*Figure 114. **The nobleman returns from afar and makes an accounting***

In the last chapter we heard about Christ's glorious Resurrection; now let us hear how he plans to sit in judgment. To explain his method of judging, Christ explicates a parable he taught a group of listeners when he was preaching in this world (Luke 19.12–27). He tells the story of a man about to journey to a far off land to receive another kingdom, and then to return home. He gives to his servants ten minas to invest, and when he returns home, the servants are to return the money to the master with the interest that it earned. He departs, accepts the other kingdom, returns home, and demands from each servant the loan plus the interest. He who acquires a great profit is rewarded handsomely, and he who acquires a little profit receives a smaller reward. The servant who returns the ten minas with no gain does not please the master, who then punishes him for not making a profit. Christ will judge in this manner on the day of the last judgment because he shall reward each individual according to his or her progress. Those who have made nothing will receive nothing, and will lament their negligence forever in hell. It is not sufficient that we renounce sin, but it is necessary that we perform good works. The strict judge will reap where he does not plant, looking for good works from the pagans even though no one preached to them. The strict judge expects much more from the Christian to whom he has delivered many beneficial lessons. To the sinners Christ shows his wounds, including those on his arms, from the Passion,

so they may see the torture he underwent for them. All the arms of Christ, the instruments of his Passion, confront the sinner, and all his wounds cry out for vengeance. Everyone is prepared to war against the sinner, and even all the elements plead a case against him. The earth makes a plea that she bore him and fed him, but he lived a life as useless as a sterile tree. Fire makes the complaint that it gave him light and warmth, yet he was unwilling to acknowledge his Creator, the true light. Air makes the plea that it was always ready to give him air to breathe, but he was ungrateful for so great a gift. Water makes the complaint that he had water to drink and fish to eat, but he would not take time to serve his Creator. His angel pleads that he was always prepared to protect him, but he did not fear to sin shamefully before God and in his presence. The Mother of Mercy who is prepared to help every sinner will not be his helper at this time or his advocate. Most pious Jesus, who died for sinners at this time of judgment, will laugh at the destruction of the damned. The demons will reveal every sin, even the hidden ones, and the angels will recite good works not done. Now the most dutiful Jesus will judge so strictly that neither prayers nor tears will change the sentence. Even if Mary and all the saints cry tears of blood, the tears are not influential enough to free one of the damned.

Chapter 29

Figure 115. **The kingdom of Heaven is like the ten virgins**

Figure 116. **The hand of God writes on the wall**

The severity of the strict judge is demonstrated in the parable of the ten virgins, which is found in the Gospels (Matthew 25.1–12). The prudent virgins will not cooperate with the foolish ones and are thus unwilling to share their oil with them. In fact, they adamantly refuse to give them oil, and even rejoice in the fate of the foolish virgins. They mock and insult their foolish sisters and tell them to go to a merchant to purchase oil. They act just as the blessed will act, mocking the damned and sending them to a merchant saying, "You have sold eternal joy for worthless pleasures, now go to your merchant and buy more fleeting delights! All the alms you gave and all the good works you did, you have sold for praise and vainglory. What are pride and vainglory doing for you now? Where are the pleasures and glories of yesteryear? See how much all the good works you sold are valued now! See how much all the fleeting gifts you received profit you now!" After the foolish virgins receive no mercy from their prudent sisters, they immediately seek out the spouse, who also shows them no mercy in his judgment: "Amen, I say to you, I do not know you!" So it likewise happens to the sinners on judgment day, for they do not receive mercy from God nor from his saints. This manner of judging is also found in another place in the Scriptures when the hand of the Lord writes on the wall in opposition to King Balthassar:

Mane, Thechel, Phares. The words are translated to mean: number, weight, and division. The judgment of God is considered under the aspect of number, and weight, and is completed by division or separation of evil from good. The Lord will judge everyone according to the number of his sins because our every deed and every word are counted. The Lord knows all our thoughts and actions, and every time we think or act, he knows the outcome. He counts all the gifts we receive, knows how we use them, and how long we possess them. All our words and deeds are counted and weighed in a balance. Then he shows to all what their value might be. A poor man's modest coin will weigh as much as 1,000 talents of gold of a Pope or an Emperor. One eggshell of gold without the burden of a deadly sin will weigh more than an infinite amount of gold weighed down with the deadly sins. One Lord's Prayer said with devotion weighs more than the recitation of the entire Psalter without attention. Finally, we consider the word "Phares" or division because the damned are divided and separated from the fellowship of God and the saints, and then proceed with the demons to Hell. The blessed now enter into the everlasting joy. Jesus Christ, King of Heaven, who is blessed forever and ever with the Father and the Holy Spirit, deems us worthy and leads us to the heavenly kingdom!

INTERPRETING THE BLOCKBOOK

INTERPRETATION AND COMMENTARY

Chapter 1

Figure 1. The Fall of Lucifer

The first illustration and commentary focus on three biblical passages that recount the fall of Lucifer: Isaias 14.12–15, 2 Peter 2.4, and the Apocalypse 12.7–9. The illustration shows the expulsion of the fallen angels during the war in Heaven. With lances and swords, four good angels, two on either side of God, overpower four evil angels. Three of the evil angels descend headlong from the wall surrounding Heaven, and the fourth appears to be in a state of free fall, feet downward. Below, the gaping jaws of Hell, visualized as a fire-breathing monster, open upward, having already encompassed two fallen angels and anticipating the added four. The mouth of Hell has large pointed teeth, curved inward, for piercing the victims and rows of smaller teeth for biting them. From the center of the outstretched jaws, flames emerge to scorch the fallen angels. The text from Isaias in the Vulgate refers to the primary fallen angel as "Lucifer," which means "bearer of light," whose descent is variously described: as the morning star or daystar fallen from the firmament and cast onto the earth, as the aspirant who sought to rival the godhead by establishing a throne on high and whose ironic and fit retribution was to have been consigned to the bottom of the abyss. The text from Peter's epistle recounts that the fallen angels after their defeat inhabited dark underground caves. The text from the Apocalypse describes the war in Heaven in which Michael and the good angels prevail over the dragon and his angels, so that the vanquished were hurled downward onto the earth. The dragon signifies the opponent of the godhead, called not only the devil, which means "doer of evil" or "foe of goodness," but also Satan, whose name, from the Hebrew, means "adversary."

Figure 2. God created man in his own image and likeness

Genesis 2.18–24 is the basis of the second illustration and commentary, in which God strives to create a suitable helpmate for Adam. Eve emerges from a cleavage in the right side of Adam, who is asleep on a hillock. With her right hand being clasped by the left hand of God the Father, who faces her, Eve is being elevated, fully formed, from Adam. With his right hand, God, likened to a gardener or planter, issues a blessing, while Eve's left hand is uplifted and outstretched to accept the Father's benediction. The fertile natural landscape implies that Adam and Eve will propagate their species, in accordance with the divine enjoinder to increase and multiply. In the background the trees may include the Tree of Life and the Tree of Knowledge of Good and Evil, the only trees named in the Garden of Eden. The illustrator may be suggesting that the eventual ruination and then the redemption of humankind will take place at the sites of trees. And though the Tree of Life in the Garden of Eden is not the site of the redemption of humankind, typically religious authors, like the seventeenth century English poet George Herbert, cite the cross as the "tree of life to all." The implication of such an assertion is that humankind, by partaking of the fruit of the forbidden tree, caused their own ruination. But Christ crucified projects at least a twofold significance for sacramental celebration: first, the issuance of water and blood from the cleavage in his side signifies the so-called mystical origin of Baptism and the Eucharist; second, the redeemer when figuratively likened to the fruit of a tree, including at times a stalk of grapes in the winepress of the cross, provides the repast and drink that regenerate fallen humankind. In this illustration of the creation under the aegis of the Father, the Providential irony may be the dramatic foreshadowing of the role of the Son as recreator, who reenacts, indeed fulfills, the role of the Father as creator, gardener, and planter.

Figure 3. You will eat of all the trees of Paradise

This illustration and commentary derive, in part, from Genesis 2. 22–25. After God had created Eve from the side of Adam, he brought the woman to the man. In the illustration God the Father, who wears a cape, appears to be officiating at a quasi-liturgical celebration of marriage, at which the right hands of the participants are about to be conjoined. Genesis 2.25 comments on the nakedness of Adam and Eve, though the husband and wife felt no shame in each other's presence. The fertile setting in which God conjoins Adam and Eve highlights the bounty of his creation intended for humankind; over all of it they will preside, and they may partake of much of it for sustenance. Not to be overlooked is the aptness of the fertile setting for God's enjoinder in Genesis 1.18: that Adam and Eve should increase and multiply, a divine command to propagate their species.

Before the creation of Eve, however, God the Father instructed Adam that he might eat of all the trees in the garden, with the exception of the Tree of Knowledge of Good and Evil (Genesis 2.16–17). Presumably, Adam in due course imparts this admonition to Eve. In Genesis 3.1–3, she, while separated from Adam, emphasizes the divine prohibition to the serpent-tempter. Eve's separation, however it came about, seems to violate both the means of her creation and the nature of her union with Adam. In fact, the separation is tantamount to conjugal disunion. Issuing from Adam's side and uplifted by the hand of God the Father, her creator and artificer, Eve is to maintain, presumably, a collateral relationship with Adam. That is, having issued from his side, she was to have remained alongside Adam; and when their hands were conjoined in marriage by God, this gesture likewise signified their mutuality, not separation or independence. Alone, Eve is more vulnerable to the serpent-tempter.

Figure 4. You shall never die, but you will be like the Lord and know good and evil

The fourth illustration and commentary reflect Genesis 3.1–6, or Eve's interaction with the serpent-tempter. With her right hand, Eve appears to be identifying the one tree whose fruit she may not eat. With her left hand, she touches her stomach, apparently to call attention to her hunger, which may not be alleviated by the forbidden fruit. While she may be in a state of hunger, her physical condition also signifies a psychological appetite or sinful desire that the serpent-tempter whets by urging her to be godlike. Opposite Eve and on the other side of the interdicted tree is the serpent-tempter. The elements of its appearance — the face of a woman, the body of a serpent, ribbed wings associated with the fallen angels, and the legs and talons of a bird of prey — all suggest a fabulous animal, a congeries of disharmony that identifies the creature as unnatural, surely not God's handiwork. The serpent-tempter assumes the face of a woman who resembles Eve. This mirror image is her alter ego, which reflects her transgressive nature. In her own discourse, Eve articulates obedience to God's command against partaking of the forbidden fruit; but from the discourse of her mirror image, or alter ego, Eve hears a challenge to God's command and accepts as valid the purported reason for the divine prohibition: God so covets his divinity that he denies that very state to humankind, who can attain to it by partaking of the interdicted fruit. A classical analogue of Eve's encounter with a mirror image of herself is the myth of Narcissus. If, therefore, Eve's desire to be godlike manifests inordinate self-love and vainglory, then her impulses when enacted may be classified as Narcissistic. Just as Narcissus died when he grasped at the mirror image of himself in a pool of water, so too Eve brings about ruination — the mutability that leads to physical death and the sinfulness that causes spiritual death — when she acts to achieve the godlike image of herself that the serpent-tempter espouses.

Chapter 2

Figure 5. Eve deceives Adam to eat with her

Genesis 3.6–7 underlies the fifth illustration and commentary, for Eve having received the forbidden fruit from the serpent-tempter has shared it, in turn, with Adam. That is, Scripture recounts that Eve partook of the forbidden fruit, then gave some to Adam, who eats of it at her behest. The illustration depicts the serpent-tempter with a forbidden fruit in its mouth, a fruit about to be transferred to Eve's outstretched left hand. Though Adam, in short, does not directly confront the serpent-tempter, who faces only Eve, he nevertheless becomes corrupted through Eve's mediation. The serpent-tempter no longer appears with a human head, perhaps to suggest that the mirror image of Eve by which she herself was seduced has served its purpose. The emphasis here is on the seduction of Adam, which is achieved by Eve, not by the serpent-tempter. Scripture also recounts that Adam and Eve, while experiencing shame after they become acutely aware of their nakedness, cover themselves with fig leaves. Both of them in the illustration use their right hands to do so, while their left hands hold forbidden fruits. Another reason for the more natural form of the serpent entwined upright along the tree is to develop ironic contrast with Christ crucified. Whereas the serpent provides a repast that results in death, Christ crucified offers the Eucharistic banquet from the tree of life to all. Furthermore, countering the trope of the upright evil serpent is the sign of the brazen serpent uplifted on a pole by Moses (Numbers 21.6–9), an action that revives the Israelites who had been stung by the so-called fiery serpents. In John 3.13–15, Jesus, who anticipates his own elevation on the cross, recalls the episode of the uplifted serpent in the desert. He avers that the Son of Man must be lifted up after the manner of the brazen serpent so that the faithful may gain salvation.

Figure 6. An angel with a flaming sword cast Adam and Eve from the garden

Genesis 3.23–24, which describes the expulsion from the Garden of Eden, furnishes the context here. An angel with a flaming sword banishes Adam and Eve from Paradise. As they exit, fig leaves conceal their nakedness. Adam elevates his left hand in a gesture of solemn and sad farewell. The angel with the sword resembles the victors similarly armed in the war in Heaven and the expulsion of the fallen angels. Whereas the angel of expulsion wields a fiery sword, the punitive fires in the illustration of the war in Heaven issue from the mouth of Hell. As Adam and Eve step beyond the wall of Paradise and outside its gate, the terrain resembles the Garden of Eden. As they will soon discover, however, the earth has become inhospitable, and tilling the ground will be a chore. The major significance of this illustration is that it typifies the retributive judgment of the godhead, whether against the fallen angels or fallen humankind, though of course the latter have opportunities for regeneration. If such opportunities are rejected, then the damnation of fiery incarceration awaiting unregenerate humankind is akin to what befell the evil angels. Such damnation will be imparted after the Second Coming and the General Resurrection and at the Final Judgment. Associated with damnation are the sword of justice and the fires of retribution. In contrast to such a retributive and punitive judgment stands the merciful judgment that the regenerate will receive after having accepted the offer of salvation. For the regenerate, the Final Judgment will unite them with, not alienate them from, the godhead, whose countenance will not be wrathful, but compassionate and merciful. Ultimately the regenerate will rest at the bosom of the Lord.

Figure 7. Here Adam with sweat on his brow delves the earth

The seventh illustration and commentary center on the aftermath of the fall of Adam and Eve and the Lord's punishment of them as recounted in Genesis 3.16–19: The woman will undergo pain in childbearing, as well as in actual birth; the man will labor to till the soil and in so doing will have sweat on his brow even as he eats. The illustration highlights Eve's domesticity, for she has a child seated on her right knee, and with her hands she is spinning. That is, a distaff with flax or wool is upright to her left; and with her left hand she guides the thread across her lap and onto a spindle under her right hand. Adam with a shovel is delving into the soil and breaking it into clods, which will be disintegrated further in pre-paration for seeding. The respective duties of Adam and Eve dra-matize their division of labor. In several respects, this visualization of the "first family" supplies a context for later illustrations of the "holy family" of Jesus, Mary, and Joseph. Adam and Eve may be contrasted with Joseph and Mary, respectively. The child on Eve's right knee presumably is Cain, the older of her two sons, who may be contrasted with the Christ child. Not to be overlooked is the Lord's rejection of Cain's sacrifice, whereas the sacrifice of Jesus at the crucifixion elicits God the Father's approbation. Christ's sacri-fice resembles Abel's, which gained the Lord's acceptance. More-over, like Abel, who was slain by his brother, Christ falls victim to the enmity of his adversaries. Further irony derives from the recog-nition that Eve, in the illustration, is nurturing the son who will murder the second son, another enactment of death in the human condition, which was initiated at the downfall of humankind. The corruption from the first sin of humankind proliferates through their descendants.

Figure 8. The Ark of Noe

The eighth illustration and commentary elaborate on Genesis 6.8–12, when, after the deluge, Noe releases from the ark first a raven, then a dove to learn whether the waters receded from the surface of the earth. The raven flew back and forth, between the ark and the flooded earth, until the waters receded, at which time it did not re-turn to Noe. Presumably, the raven, a carnivore with a "ravenous" appetite, was awaiting the appearance of carcasses on the mountaintops, after which it began to feed. Thereafter, Noe released a dove, an herbivore, which returned because it found no place on which to alight and to feed. Released seven days later, the dove returned with an olive branch in its beak, indicating natural growth on earth. After being released for the third time, the dove did not return to the ark.

The commentary on the illustration interprets the olive branch as a sign of God's mercy, not only to Noe and his family in the ark but also to humankind who experience salvation. Advancing this interpretation, one may note that the olive branch, a traditional emblem of peace, signifies the renewed harmony between humankind and the godhead after the deluge. The crushed olive and its oil represent Christ crucified and the life-giving consequences of that sacrifice for humankind. The dove, a gentle bird, typifies the merciful countenance of the Lord after his wrath, which was manifested in the cataclysmic deluge of unregenerate humankind, has been satisfied. The Lord is also appeased by the sacrifice of Jesus on behalf of humankind. The dove, moreover, is an emblem of the Holy Spirit, whose return to the ark foreshadows its visit to embolden and enlighten the disciples at Pentecost, for Noe, like the disciples, preaches on behalf of the Lord. In its appearance, moreover, the ark resembles a temple or place of worship, a place of security in the midst of the tempest-tossed sea and the vicissitudes of the human condition. Accordingly, Noe and his family typify the community of believers who, despite adversity, maintain their faith, patience, and fortitude, thereby foreshadowing the role of the disciples who, after Pentecost, will suffer many travails as they preach on the Lord's behalf at the ends of the earth.

Chapter 3

Figure 9. Here the birth of Mary is announced

The ninth illustration and commentary, which present the genealogy of the Virgin Mary, are ultimately derived from extra-canonical books of Scripture, the apocryphal gospels. Probably, however, the more proximate source was the *Legenda Aurea* or the *Golden Legend* (ca. 1260–1270) by Jacobus de Voragine, which summarizes the accounts in the New Testament apocrypha. The illustration shows an angel announcing to Joachim the conception and eventual birth of the Virgin Mary to his wife, Anna (see *The Golden Legend or Lives of the Saints*, trans. William Caxton [The Temple Classics: London, 1900; rpt. New York, 1973], vol. 5, 99–101). Joachim of the tribe of Judah had gone to the Temple to make offerings to the Lord, but a scribe scolded him as childless, stigmatized him as unblessed, and designated him as unfit to offer sacrifices. Dispirited, Joachim fled to the mountains and lived among shepherds and their flocks. In the ninth illustration, Joachim still bearing the receptacle with his offerings encounters an angel of the Lord, who announces that Anna will conceive and give birth to a daughter, who will be sanctified. Within view of Joachim and the angel are a shepherd and his flock, suggesting resemblance to the scene of the Nativity of Jesus, his role as the Good Shepherd, and his identification as a lamb for sacrifice.

Such a significant setting is an appropriate context for the announcement (or annunciation) of the conception and imminent birth of the mother of Jesus. Since sheep are meek and mild and serve as sacrificial offerings in Scripture, they signify the self-abnegation of Mary and Christ, both of whom are obedient to the will of the Father and to his Providential plan for salvation. The announcement of Mary's birth is extraordinary, for she is especially chosen by God to be the sinless vessel through whom the Son will be born with a human nature and form. This incarnation of the Son is necessary for his mission and ministry — the Savior whose redemptive death offers eternal life to humankind. Fittingly, the commentary on the illustration, in referring to a well-known parable in Scripture (the Good Samaritan), lauds Christ as the protector and healer of humankind, as the fulfillment of the merciful service of the Good Samaritan (Luke 10.29–36). In line with this interpretation, Mary is perceived as having made Christ available, a protecting

and healing agent whose salutary effect is to revive humankind who
are dead in spirit.

Figure 10. King Astyages has an extraordinary dream

Another extra-biblical source for the *Mirror of Human Salvation* is
Historia Scholastica by Petrus Comestor, who died around 1179. In
Historica Scholastica (*Patrologia Latina*, CXCVIII, 1470), Comestor
recounts the dream of King Astyages concerning his daughter, the
basis for the tenth illustration and commentary. In the illustration,
the daughter stands at the foot of her father's bed. From her chest
and evidently at her heart, the stalk of a vine emerges, and along
with it branches, leaves, and clusters of fruit, probably grapes. As
part of the dream-vision, the fruit-bearing vine covered King
Astyages's entire realm. The interpretation of the dream as reported to King Astyages centered upon the imminent birth of a son
to his daughter. That son, who became King Cyrus, liberated the
Israelites from their Babylonian captivity (1 Esdras 1). In doing so,
he rebuilt the Temple of Yahweh in Jerusalem and returned to it
the sacred vessels that King Nabuchodonosor had plundered. While
the commentary focuses on the historical significance of King
Astyages's dream, it glances at the so-called mystical interpretation of the same event. Consistent with the overall theme of chapter 3, the daughter of the king signifies the Virgin Mary, from whom
will issue forth figuratively the grape vine that will cover the earth.
Evident in the illustration and commentary is the Virgin Mary's
implied typological resemblance to Noe, who was the first to plant
the grape vine (Genesis 9.20), and to his descendants, who popu-
lated the earth. In the Christian dispensation, the fruit of the vine,
of course, is the *bon fruit* of the Virgin Mary's womb, Jesus. When
squeezed in the winepress of the cross, that fruit supplies the saving grace that sacramentally liberates humankind from the forces
of Satan, sin, and death.

Figure 11. An enclosed garden, a sealed fountain

This illustration and commentary hearken back to the Canticle of Canticles (4.12), in which the lover celebrates his beloved as a garden enclosed and a sealed fountain. Attributed to Solomon, the Canticle of Canticles is a series of love poems or hymns in which the speaker woos his bride. Often interpreted allegorically, as the Lord's loving union with Israel, or Christ's marriage to the church, tropes and images from the Canticle of Canticles were also used in Marian devotions. Litanies extolled the Virgin Mary as the immaculate spouse of the Lord and as the veritable salvatrix of humankind because she was the conduit through which the Son entered the human condition. Celebrated variously as the bride, mother, and daughter of the Lord, the Virgin Mary assumes spousal, maternal, and filial significance in her manifold relationship with the godhead. The images of the enclosed garden and sealed fountain elaborate on her significance in various ways. The word "paradise," with its Persian etymology, means "walled or enclosed garden." Whereas the paradisal Garden of Eden was breached by the serpent-tempter, the Virgin Mary, figured by the walled or enclosed garden, remains impervious to the onset of evil. As the so-called second Eve, the Virgin manifests an uncorrupt and incorruptible *hortus mentis* or garden of the mind, whereas Eve yielded to the seduction of the serpent-tempter. Likened to a sealed fountain, secure from sinful pollution, the Virgin is the wellspring and conduit for the saving grace that issues from the Son's presence in the human condition. The word "sealed" connotes the source of grace contained in her womb, its implantation there by divine approval and the acceptance by the Virgin Mary. At the Annunciation by the angel Gabriel, Mary's acceptance that she will become the mother of Jesus — "Be it done unto me according to thy word" (Matthew 1.38) — in effect seals the covenant with the godhead. Not to be overlooked is the resemblance of the fountain in the illustration to a baptismal fount, whose waters when released provide the seal of the sacrament of initiation.

Figure 12. Balaam through a star prophesied the birth of Mary

The account of Balaam appears in Numbers 22–24. Known for his curses and blessings, Balaam was entreated by Balac, king of Moab, to visit him. By donkey, Balaam traveled to Moab, but the animal, seeing the angel of the Lord with a drawn sword, veered off the road. When Balaam beat the donkey, it resumed its travel, but the angel blocked the roadway, and the animal stopped in its tracks. Prodded by another beating, the animal continued, until the third interruption, when the donkey is made to speak by Yahweh. When Balaam finally saw the angel with the drawn sword, he fell to the ground, prostrate and penitential. Admonished by the angel to speak only what Yahweh tells him to say, Balaam continues his journey to Moab. There, when enjoined by Balac to curse the Israelites, God tells Balaam to bless the chosen people. In a series of lyrical poems, rhapsodic in tone, Balaam extols the Israelites. Accompanying the ninth illustration, the commentary notes a prophetic allusion to the Virgin Mary — "a star from Jacob" — in one of the lyrical poems. This epithet describes the Virgin Mary as *Stella Maris* or "Star of the Sea." Allegorically, she is the guide for vessels traveling the tempest-tossed seas of the present life and seeking direction heavenward. The prophetic star having presaged her birth, as well as her role as a beacon to travelers, the Virgin Mary, after the manner of Balaam's transformation of a curse into a blessing, will function as the Second Eve, so that "Eva" will give way to "Ave."

The Virgin Mary, in effect, will counteract the curse on humankind that resulted from Eve's transgression, for a blessing will befall humankind through her mediation. The commentary cites one of the miracles of the Virgin as a dramatic example of her role as a guide and beacon to humankind and her power to transform a curse into a blessing. In a popular medieval legend, Theophilus of Cilicia had contracted in writing with the devil, exchanging his soul after death for worldly power. Suffering remorse, he prayed to the Virgin Mary, who pardoned him and then wrested from the devil the written agreement, which she returned to Theophilus, who made a public confession and died in a sanctified state.

Chapter 4

Figure 13. The nativity of the glorious Virgin Mary

Ultimately from the apocryphal gospels, particularly the Prot-evangelium of James, and summarized, in turn, in *Legenda Aurea* or *Golden Legend*, the birth of the Virgin Mary is featured in the thirteenth illustration and commentary. (See Voragine, vol. 5, 101.) In the illustration, Joachim returns the infant Mary to her mother, Anna, who lies in bed after having recently given birth to the child. Citing Isaias 11.1–2, which centers on the Tree of Jesse, the genealogy of Mary is traced to the House of David. The Virgin ("virgo" in Latin) is likened to the rod or branch ("virga" in Latin), which emerges from the root of Jesse, the father of David. As the rod or branch, she will bear the flower — Jesus — that issues from the same root or ancestry. The glancing reference to the heavenly dew that will make the rod fruitful implies awareness of another biblical text, Judges 6.36–38, which recounts how Gedeon sought a sign of military victory from the Lord. When Gedeon placed a woolen fleece on a dry floor, and the fleece became moist while its surroundings did not, he took this phenomenon as a sign of impend-ing victory. The sign traditionally prefigures the impregnation of the Virgin Mary at the Annunciation, when the godhead infuses her with grace; and the victory that Mary and her Christ child achieve pertains to their freedom from sinfulness and the liberation from sinfulness that they offer humankind.

Most significant in the commentary are the medicinal properties associated with the flower that grows from the branch — or with the Christ child who issues from the Virgin Mary. The seven remedies from the flower, which engage the maladies of the soul, are anti-dotes to the seven deadly sins. Having originated with the Virgin

Mary and Christ, these remedies become the gifts of the Holy Spirit, which are available to humankind.

Figure 14. A branch will spring from the root of Jesse

Both the fourteenth illustration and commentary elaborate on the significance of the Tree of Jesse. The illustration shows Jesse asleep in a chair, resembling a throne, probably because the faces and busts of some of the figures are kings that constitute the family tree of Jesus. Resembling the stalk, vine, and branches that emerge from the daughter of King Astyages, the Tree of Jesse at its summit features the Virgin Mary enthroned, with the Christ child on her lap. The kings, as well as prophets and patriarchs who appear in the Tree of Jesse, are included in two catalogs in Scripture, both of which outline the genealogy of Christ. The first catalog enumerates the descendants of Noe by his son Sem (Genesis 11.10–32); the second catalog, which prefaces Matthew's Gospel, cites the ancestors of Christ, highlighting Abraham and David but also mentioning Isaac, Jacob, and, of course, Jesse.

Most significant in the commentary on the illustration is what may be called an anatomy of the Tree of Jesse — its seven parts and their appeal to sensory perception. The commentator correlates each part with a remedy for a particular malady of the soul or for one of the deadly sins. The remedies, while attributed to Christ, are also correlated with the seven gifts of the Holy Spirit, which, when provided to humankind, will restore spiritual well-being. The uppermost vine on which the Virgin and Christ child are enthroned resembles the arch across the vault of the heavens where Christ will be seated at the Second Coming. At times, this arch resembles a rainbow, whose significance is at least twofold: the promise of God not to destroy the world again by water, and the manifestation of mercy by God after the punitive deluge satisfied his justice. If indeed the rainbow-throne is suggested, then the illustration anticipates Christ in session at the Second Coming, when fire, not water, will engulf the world. From his throne, Christ may issue a judgment of damnation or of salvation.

Figure 15. The closed door signifies the Blessed Virgin Mary

The fifteenth illustration and commentary derive from the vision of Ezechiel (Ezechiel 44.1–3), who views the sanctuary, specifically the outer gate or door facing eastward. He learns that the Lord has entered the sanctuary in this way, and that the gate or door has been shut after his entry, never to be used by another. In the commentary, the closed door comes to signify the Virgin Mary inside whom Christ, the flower, grew and blossomed secretly. Mary, therefore, is likened to the "sanctum sanctorum" or "holy of holies," the bearer of the Logos or the Divine Word. Thus, the wonder and mystery of the virginal birth of Jesus are unique, never to be reenacted. The closed door represents, as well, Mary's continuous virginity — before and after the birth of Christ. The inviolate presence of Christ inside Mary, an inviolable vessel, signifies "Mater Ecclesia" and the Lord's dwelling therein. To be sure, an external edifice or so-called "house of God" comes to mind, but the commentary speaks more about a fit habitation for the Lord in the human heart and the purgation that must be achieved before this indwelling takes place. Emphasized in the commentary is the power of discernment whereby humankind, having received the seven remedies associated with Christ and with the Gifts of the Holy Spirit, will see, know, and understand that the eternal realm will prevail over the temporal domain. As this perception takes hold, and the seven deadly sins or their potential development are systematically purged by spiritual antidotes, then the Lord may choose to enter such a human heart and sanctify it by his presence. The effect is to imprint the Divine Word and godlike image on the human heart and to bear Jesus within oneself, a process of indwelling whereby one is transformed by and into the very presence at the core of one's nature.

Figure 16. The Temple of Solomon signifies the Blessed Mary

The sixteenth illustration and commentary present the temple of Solomon, described in 3 Kings 6.8, as an image of the Virgin Mary.

The features of the temple, both pictured and recounted, are correlated with events in the life of the Virgin Mary and with her
attributes. In this extended allegorical correlation, at least the following events in her life are cited: her own birth, her motherhood of
Jesus, and her relationship with the evangelists and apostles. Thus,
the three pinnacles of the temple suggest the triple crown of Mary,
each horn of gold with its particular significance — her virginity,
her martyrdom in spirit, and her lofty status as a role model for
teachers and preachers, particularly the evangelists and apostles.
Whereas her virginity is self-evident, the martyrdom of Mary derives from her spirit of self-abnegation and her empathetic death at
the crucifixion of Jesus, whom she accompanies to the foot of the
cross. Her service as a role model refers to interaction with the
evangelists, whose accounts of the infancy, childhood, adolescence,
and early adulthood of Christ presumably derive from Mary. Scripture documents, moreover, Mary's interaction with the apostles,
whose company she kept (Acts of the Apostles 1.14), perhaps even
at Pentecost (Acts 2.1–41). In addition, her own birth and life, on
the one hand, and the birth and life of Jesus, on the other, are celebrated in the appearance of the exterior and interior of the temple
of Solomon. Constructed of "dazzling white marble," the exterior
represents the purity and chastity of the Virgin Mary, whereas the
interior, made of gold, signifies "the most precious charity" of Jesus.
Finally, the ladder used to climb upward in the temple represents
the means that Mary provides for humankind to ascend to heavenly glory.

Chapter 5

Figure 17. In the temple Mary is presented to the Lord

From the apocryphal gospels, particularly the Protevangelium of
James, but also recounted in *Legenda Aurea* or *Golden Legend*, the
Presentation of the Virgin Mary is the topic of the seventeenth
illustration and commentary. (see Voragine, vol. 5, 101–02.) At the

viewer's left, Anna and Joachim have placed the Virgin Mary, three
years old, atop an altar in the temple. At the right the chief priest
welcomes the child to a life of study and service to God. Despite her
youth, the Virgin Mary appears to be adult-like in appearance,
though not in stature, as if the godhead already imparted dignity
and maturity to her because of her selection to be the mother of
Jesus. Already, even though a child, she, like Jesus, who as a youth
instructed the rabbis in the temple, seems dignified and mature
beyond her years. Indeed, while her parents are presenting Mary to
the chief priest, she, in effect, stands above them all, as they gaze
upward toward her.

With her hands extended downward, she appears to be in the
attitude typical of her statues, statuettes, and paintings, which portray her as the recipient of prayers and petitions from humankind.
As an intercessor, patroness, and advocate, the Virgin Mary en-
dorses those prayers and petitions, offering them on behalf of humankind to the godhead. Above her parents and the chief priest,
the Virgin Mary even as a child anticipates her elevated status —
a model for emulation by humankind and a specially elected human being with proximity to the godhead. The commentary on this
illustration is from the legend of the table of the sun. (See Valerius
Maximus, *Valerii Maximi Factorum et Dictorum Memorabilium
Libri Novem*, ed. C. Halm [Leipzig: Teubner Classics, 1865], bk. 4,
chapter 1, ext. 7.) Referring to a "wondrous stroke of good fortune"
that befell fishermen who cast their net into the sea, the legend
records that they elevated in it "a precious and exceedingly beautiful table made of pure gold and whose beauty was evident to all
who saw it." Transporting it to the temple of the god of the sun, the
fishermen show the table to a priest, who presumably will designate it as the place whereon sacred vessels will be kept for use in
the sacrifices at the altar nearby. Used in this way, the table becomes the counterpart of the one specified by the Lord in Exodus
25.23–30 as a furnishing in the sanctuary. Allegorically, the table
of the sun signifies the Virgin Mary, who at her Presentation was
consecrated as the sacred vessel to bear Christ, who will be sacrificed on the altar of the cross.

Figure 18. The golden table in the sand is presented in the temple of the sun

Continuing the story of the golden table, the eighteenth illustration and commentary show two fishermen still wearing their boots but paying homage in the temple of the god of the sun. In the presence of a priest, the fisherman to the left still carries his net, while the one at the right holds the table as an offering. On the altar is a statue of the god of the sun standing upright and holding, in the one hand, a lance with a pennon and, in the other, a shield on which appears the face of the sun. In many ways, the god anticipates the risen Christ in his triumphant attitude. The illustration features the interplay of the table and the sacrifice, with Mary likened to the former and Christ to the latter.

Their implied relationship involves the role of the table, which signifies Mary, in bearing and bringing the offering, namely Christ, to the altar. A corollary of this implied relationship is the idea of Christ as the heavenly food or banquet, a resemblance underscoring his own comments in John's Gospel on the "bread of life," notably of eternal life. The sacramental implications of the "body and blood" of Jesus borne and transported by the Virgin dramatize the quasi-ministerial role of Mary in presenting the offering to the godhead. That is, Christ's sacrificial and redemptive mission and ministry become possible because Mary invests the Son with human nature and form, the prerequisites of his sacrifice. The commentary dwells chiefly on the one other instance in Scripture wherein a parent or parents offered a child to God. Citing Jephte and his daughter (Judges 11.31–39), the commentary explains systematically how and why that action differs from Joachim and Anna's presentation of their daughter, Mary, to God.

Figure 19. Jephte sacrifices his daughter to the Lord

In the nineteenth illustration and commentary, Jephte implements his agreement with the Lord: If he were granted victory over the Ammonites, he would sacrifice the first person who met him from his own home after he returns from battle. At his victorious home-coming, the first person who comes forward to meet him is his daughter, an only child. Grieving at his vow, Jephte nevertheless agrees to sacrifice his daughter. In the nineteenth illustration, he, on horseback and at the head of his army, wields his sword against his daughter, who kneels on the ground before him. Continuing the contrast between Jephte and Mary's parents, the commentary cites two added major differences: Jephte's victory was over temporal forces, another army, whereas Mary's triumph is eternal; Jephte by sacrificing his daughter eliminated any further service she could have performed, but Mary's service to the Lord extends forever. Concerning the first difference, Mary's eternal triumph, unlike Jephte's victory over another tribe, cannot be overestimated be-cause, through Christ, the forces of Satan, sin, and darkness, the most formidable adversaries of humankind, are defeated forever. Thus, the self-abnegation of Mary's parents, of Mary herself, and of Christ may be contrasted with Jephte's self-interest. Having negotiated with the Lord, and having stipulated circumstances under which he would offer sacrifice (his victory over adversaries) Jephte is tainted by pride; for he does not give himself over to the Lord in the spirit of unconditional service. Concerning the second difference, Mary's service to the Lord continues even after the death of Christ. She is among the disciples while they are initiating their ministry to disseminate Christ's message, and she remains the patroness and intercessor for the faithful until the Second Coming.

Figure 20. From atop the hanging garden, the Queen of Persia sees her homeland

The twentieth illustration and commentary deal with the Queen of Persia, who resides in a tower. Characterized in Peter Comestor's *Historia Scholastica* (*Patrologia Latina*, CXCVIII, 1453), the Queen of Persia is traditionally likened to the Virgin Mary. In the process of developing this correlation, the commentary on the illustration cites the Canticle of Canticles 5.2: "I sleep, but my heart is vigilant." This passage anticipates the parable of the five wise and foolish virgins (Matthew 25.1–13). Because of her vigilance, the Queen of Persia wards off unwariness. Likewise, the Virgin Mary after her Presentation remains ready to heed the call of the Lord and to serve him. By vigilantly keeping a supply of oil for their torches, the five wise virgins prepare themselves to meet the groom at midnight. In a larger context, to be sure, being attentive and ready typifies the faithful who await the Lord at the Second Coming, or await more immediately the moment of their death in a spiritual state of holiness. In the ceremonial purification of her homeland, the Queen of Persia resembles the Virgin Mary who, in giving birth to Christ, plays a major role in the process of purging and regenerating fallen humankind.

The traits of the Queen of Persia cited in the commentary on the illustration also pertain to the Virgin Mary. In effect, the composite traits indicate that the Virgin Mary, from the time of her Presentation, led a life of study and service to God. Among other things, fixing one's eyes on the ground but elevating one's heart heavenward typify the attitude of the Virgin Mary in most visual depictions; for modesty, humility, and the profession of one's unworthiness are all indicated. Not to be overlooked in the illustration is the enclosure that surrounds the tower, which protects it and its environs, a garden, from defilement. This enclosure or walled garden reflects a place of continuous holiness, including the interiority of the Virgin — her mind, heart, and soul.

Chapter 6

Figure 21. Here the Virgin Mary marries Joseph

A priest officiates at the marriage of Mary and Joseph, a tableau resembling the marriage of Adam and Eve under the aegis of the godhead. The scriptural account of the relationship of Mary and Joseph occurs in Matthew 1.18–25. But the apocryphal gospels provide further legendary accounts concerning the process whereby a spouse was chosen for Mary. In the commentary on the illustration, eight reasons, presented from a Providential perspective, are cited for the marriage of Mary, all of which (with one exception) focus on her, rather than on Joseph. This emphasis on Mary harmonizes with one of the overall themes of the present blockbook: her role as God's specially chosen virgin to be the mother of Jesus, her ongoing service to God even after the temporal ministry of her son, the perception by humankind of her and her service, and their ongoing relationship with Mary as patroness, intercessor, heavenly queen. The one exception among the eight reasons for Mary's marriage to Joseph centers on the cultural practice of tracing a child's genealogy through the father. The genealogy of Jesus, traced through Joseph or "the husband of Mary" (Matthew 1.16), is presented at the outset of Matthew's Gospel, immediately before the account of Mary's relationship with Joseph. The commentary infers, from other reasons for her marriage to Joseph, that Mary is the patroness and model for women who are virginal, wedded, or widowed. In this instance and in several others in the present blockbook, Mary as a model for women comes to the fore in manifold ways, anticipating their status, even as it may change in life, and upholding it, whatever it may be, as holy and dutiful.

Figure 22. Here Sara marries young Tobias

In this illustration and commentary, the marriage of Sara and Tobias (Tobias 3–7), overseen by God and, under his direction, facilitated by the angel Raphael, anticipates the God-ordained relationship of Mary and Joseph. The illustration shows the angel counseling Tobias, while her father, Raguel, gives his daughter to the young man. Tobias had doubts about Sara as a prospective wife, but with Raphael's counsel he overcomes them. One objection after another is dispelled until the betrothal and marriage ensue. To emphasize the Providential outlook on this marriage, Raphael says of Sara: "for she was set apart for you before the world existed." And while their marriage may be fruitful, Tobias is counseled that "when about to have intercourse with her, both of you first rise up to pray." Furthermore, Raphael informs Tobias that he will "save [Sara], and she will go with [him]" (Tobias 6.18). If indeed only these three admonitions are correlated with similar guidance provided to Joseph by an angel, then the Old Testament marriage serves as an insightful gloss on the one in the New Testament, specifically as recounted in Matthew's Gospel. First, like Tobias, Joseph is reluctant to accept Mary as his spouse; for he learns that she is expecting a child. An angel who appears to him in a dream-vision overcomes that objection, informing Joseph that Mary conceived a child by the Holy Spirit (Matthew 1.20). Second, Mary and Joseph, though married, "had no relations" (Matthew 1.25). Third, warned by an angel in another dream-vision, Joseph saves the Virgin Mary and the Christ child from the Massacre of the Innocents. Escaping to Egypt, Joseph and the Holy Family remain there until the death of King Herod, who issued the order for the slaying of all boys of approximately two years of age (Matthew 2.13–16).

Figure 23. The Tower called Baris signifies Mary

From Comestor's *Historia Scholastica* (*PL*, CXCVIII, 1527), the renowned tower of Baris in Egypt signifies an impregnable fortress, vigilantly protected by two sentinels, as the illustration depicts. The commentary likens the protection afforded the Virgin Mary — from the Lord above and by Joseph on earth — to the security of the tower of Baris. Continuing its exposition of the Book of Tobias, the commentary parallels Sara's chastity with that of the Virgin. Though married seven times, Sara never consummated her relationships with the men, who dropped dead as they approached her in the bridal chamber (Tobias 6.14). Slain by Asmodeus, which, from the Persian, means "demon of wrath" or "destroyer," the seven husbands never violate Sara's chastity. The commentary contends that if Asmodeus, finally exorcized by Tobias after Raphael instructed him how to do so, protected Sara, how much more did the "true God" protect the chastity of the Virgin Mary from one man — namely, Joseph. The commentary stresses that the parallel dramatizes the Virgin Mary's chastity not only during her marriage to Joseph but for her entire life. The commentary, moreover, portrays Joseph beholding the splendor of the Virgin Mary and experiencing awe.

Not unlike the radiance of Moses, who emitted light after his encounters with the Lord, the effulgence of the Virgin Mary derives from her proximity to the godhead. Favored by the Lord, she becomes a veritable "untouchable" to others. In line with the military motif evident in the tower of Baris, the commentary describes the "sovereign God" as the "safeguard" of the Virgin Mary, defending "her from every assault of the enemy." By perceiving the name "Mary" as an anagram for "army," several English religious poets — for example, George Herbert — allude to the military motif associated with the Blessed Virgin Mary, as well as with Jesus in his attitude as *Christus Victor*.

Figure 24. A thousand shields hang from the tower of David

The twenty-fourth illustration and commentary are derived from Canticles 4.4, which likens the tower of David and the 1,000 shields suspended from it to the neck of the beloved. The comparison accentuates the invincibility of the beloved, who remains untouched, and untouchable to anyone other than her lover. The commentary applies this passage from Canticles to the Virgin Mary — that the 1,000 shields represent the virtues and good works that defend her against temptation and sin. Because of the grace that she infuses in others, they too overcome sin and temptation. But the resemblance of the tower of David to the Virgin Mary centers on the manner by which the fortification and the sanctified woman disarm their prospective adversaries — that is, how they prevent adversaries from even launching an assault. In the case of the tower of David, it projects an aura of impregnability, with the shields of valorous men testifying to their fierceness as warriors. This aura would discourage would-be attackers. In the case of the Virgin Mary, no one looks on her libidinously despite her beauty. Because the commentary states that "divine power emanates from her," the Virgin Mary negates any concupiscence in a beholder. The effect of her presence is purgative and salutary to others. She becomes the site and source from which the power of sanctity vindicates goodness over evil, negates evil, and even at times transforms it to goodness; and the potency exercised through her holiness brings about a reformation of the human heart.

Chapter 7

Figure 25. The Annunciation by the angel to the Virgin Mary

Here the focus is on Matthew 1.18–21 and Luke 1.26–38, both of which recount the divine insemination of Mary at the Annunciation. In the illustration, the angel Gabriel, with his left hand, gestures in benediction toward Mary, while in his right he holds a banderole on which his utterance is recorded: "Hail full of grace, the Lord is with you." The Virgin Mary's reply, inscribed on the banderole above her, reflects humble acceptance of God's will: "Behold the handmaiden of the Lord; may it be done unto me according to your word." Because the virginal conception of Jesus occurred under the power of the Holy Spirit, Mary at the Annunciation usually appears in a locked room, for access to her is limited to the godhead or a divine emissary — namely, Gabriel. The vase in the foreground — with the water and blossoming flowers — suggests fertility, a natural image calling attention to the "fruit" of the Virgin's womb. Because of her modesty and feeling of unworthiness, Mary glances downward. At her heart Mary crosses her forearms. This gesture signifies that the Divine Word, as spoken by Gabriel and accompanied by an infusion of grace, is being impressed onto the tablet of her heart. This gesture, by its cross-like configuration, also anticipates the Virgin Mary's heartbreak, an empathetic reaction at the suffering and death of Jesus. On her lap, she has a book open presumably to Hebraic prophecies of the birth of the Messiah. In addition, the present commentary on the Annunciation interprets in a positive light the passage from Matthew 1.19–25, which describes Joseph's intention to dissociate from Mary after he learns of her pregnancy. Whereas many of the church fathers contend that

Joseph, who had had no relations with Mary, suspected her of infidelity, the present commentary highlights his affirmation of her chastity. Described as "fearing and trembling," Joseph moves to dissociate from Mary because of his own unworthiness to be near her, for he believes that she is the sacred vessel of "the divine and heavenly."

Figure 26. The Lord in the burning bush appears to Moses

While tending sheep, Moses receives from God the summons to lead the Chosen People from Egypt. At Mount Horeb, he notices a bush on fire, though it remains unconsumed (Exodus 3–4). In the illustration God, surrounded by flames, appears at the summit of a tree or bush. He extends his right hand toward Moses in a gesture of benediction, while in his left hand he holds an orb. The sign and wonder of the burning bush traditionally prefigure the mystery of Mary's motherhood of Jesus. That is, Mary becomes pregnant without having compromised her virginity. If therefore God's presence was manifested at the burning bush, it likewise radiated from within Mary, who has been inflamed with ardor and zeal for God since her Presentation. At God's command, Moses removes his footwear, because the ground at Mt. Horeb is holy. Similarly, the room in which the angel Gabriel visits Mary is a sacred space accessed only by divine approval. If the illustration correlates an account from the Old Testament, notably Moses on Mt. Horeb, with the Annunciation, so too does the commentary.

Pursuing more fully the "fearing and trembling" of Joseph, the commentary cites Old Testament prophetic accounts of the birth of the Messiah as motives for his attempted withdrawal from Mary — consider, for instance, Isaias 7.14, which recounts that a Virgin shall bear a child who shall be called Emmanuel, a name that means "God is with us." In the commentary, Joseph recalls this prophecy and others like it as the basis for his "fearing and trembling." Another prophecy likewise cited is from Isaias 11.1, which envisages the Tree of Jesse, with the Virgin as its flowering rod. Finally, the commentary also cites instances from the Old and New

Testaments where God's prophet or Jesus by his holiness causes others to feel unworthy, fearful, and awestruck.

Figure 27. Gedeon's fleece is soaked while the earth remains dry

From Judges 6.36–40, this illustration and commentary focus on Gedeon's request for a sign that the Lord will favor him in the impending battle against the Madianites, the Amalecites, and the Kedemites. Placing a woolen fleece on the threshing floor, Gedeon stipulated that if the fleece alone and not the surrounding area were moistened by dew, then this would be a sign of God's favor. Such occurred, but to seek further assurance of victory, Gedeon again placed the fleece on the threshing floor, requesting that it now remain dry while the surrounding area became moist. After the second sign of victory, Gedeon confidently entered battle and emerged triumphant.

In the illustration, Gedeon, armed for battle, kneels in prayer before the fleece, which he has placed on the slope of a hill. Droplets of heavenly dew descend from the clouds. Behind Gedeon stands an angel, whose arms outstretched toward the warrior indicate divine favor. Like Gedeon whose anxieties are relieved, Joseph also receives assurance of God's approval for him to remain with Mary. Gedeon's liberation of Israel, which the commentary likens to the deliverance of the Chosen People from Egypt, prefigures the selection of Mary as the divinely ordained abode through whom redemption would be achieved. The moistening of the fleece foreshadows Mary's impregnation; from her, Jesus will emerge to deliver humanity from the threat of damnation. If further resemblances may be developed between Gedeon's woolen fleece and the birth of the Messiah from Mary, they center on implications that Jesus is the "lamb of God" or *agnus Dei*. Because of his meekness, obedience to the will of the Father, and self-sacrifice, Jesus is aptly figured by the lamb. But after his humiliation, Jesus experiences exaltation. From *Christus Patiens* or the patient Christ enduring adversity, he becomes *Christus Victor*, triumphant over his and humankind's adversaries: Satan, sin, and darkness.

Figure 28: Rebecca gives a drink to the servant of Abraham

Derived from Genesis 24, this illustration and commentary focus on the process by which Abraham chooses a wife for his son, Isaac. Under the aegis of the Lord, Abraham instructs his senior servant to travel to the city of Nachor, to choose a wife for his son, and to return with her to Canaan. After he had arrived at Nachor, the servant prayed for a sign from the Lord: Among the daughters of the city visiting the well, whoever agreed to draw water for the servant and his camels would be Isaac's divinely selected spouse. In this manner Rebecca was chosen, and with parental approval and by her own consent, she accompanied the senior servant to Canaan. Though the illustrations show horses rather than camels, the well from which the water was drawn and the vessel in which Rebecca offers it to Abraham's servant predominate. The commentary dwells on moisture and fluids as images of spiritual sustenance or grace. Referring to the previous illustration, the commentary likens the moisture from Gedeon's fleece to the "dew of [Christ's] grace," which "fills the whole world." From this interpretation, the commentary proceeds to analyze Rebecca's offer of water to Abraham. Mary who pledges the "fount of life to the angels and to man" actually provides it by virtue of the birth of the Messiah. As the commentary states, a cup of refreshment from that fount will alleviate thirst.

Though the commentary does not cite the New Testament for an analogue of the encounter at the well, in John's Gospel Christ's discourse with the Samaritan woman parallels the meeting of Abraham's servant and Rebecca. At his return to Galilee from Judea, Jesus passed through Samaria. Stopping at Jacob's well, he requests that the Samaritan woman provide him with a drink of water. Jesus then characterizes the water from the well in the following way: that whoever drinks of it will be thirsty again. Whoever drinks of the water that he provides, however, will "never thirst"; for it will "become in him a spring of water welling up to eternal life" (John 4.14).

Chapter 8

Figure 29. The Nativity of Our Lord Jesus Christ

The nativity of the Messiah is seen here as the fulfillment of several Old Testament prophetic utterances and exhortations. Luke 2.1–7 provides the biblical account of the nativity, which is the basis for the illustration. The Christ child is at the center and in the foreground. He lies on an oval-shaped cloth, from which rays of light emanate. Often in visualizations of the Transfiguration and Resurrection, Christ in his glorification appears against an elliptically shaped backdrop, usually called a mandorla (from the Italian for almond), which radiates light. Thus, the infant Christ at his nativity is glorified, in anticipation of similar moments later in his temporal ministry. To the viewer's left is the Virgin Mary, her arms crossed over her heart, similar to her attitude at the Annunciation. To the right is Joseph, who supports himself on a walking stick, as he prepares to kneel on the ground. The walking stick becomes associated with Joseph not simply because of his profession as a carpenter but also because he leads the Virgin and Christ, both of whom typically are mounted on a donkey, into and out of Egypt. At the same time, Joseph's journey with his walking stick prefigures Jesus with his cross along the *via dolorosa*. Like Joseph, Jesus presumably fell to one or both knees during the carrying of the cross, for which weakness Simon the Cyrenian was pressed into service. But the Holy Family's journey into and out of Egypt, under Joseph's leadership, foreshadows the Paschal mystery. Egypt traditionally represents, first, the place of bondage for the Chosen People, and, second, the confines of hell. After his death and descent into, or harrowing of, hell, Jesus emerges with the multitude of his redeemed, all those who had been interned there until he fulfilled his temporal ministry. And at his Resurrection, those whom he redeemed share in his exaltation and glorification. Finally, Joseph with his right hand against his head reflects an attitude of awe and wonder because the magnitude of the mystery of redemption has begun to unfold.

Figure 30. In a dream the Pharao's cup bearer sees a vine

The thirtieth illustration and commentary center upon the dream of the Pharao's cup bearer and Joseph's interpretation of it, as recounted in Genesis 40.1–23. Incarcerated because he fell into disfavor with the Pharao, the cup bearer has a dream, which Joseph interprets as a twofold premonition — that the former servant of the Pharao will be released from the dungeon in three days, and that he will be restored to his former position. While Joseph's analysis pertains only to the dreamer, both the illustration and the commentary broaden the interpretation of the dream, whose significance may be related to humankind generally. Rather than a dungeon, the illustration shows the cup bearer in stocks, and his eyes are closed because of the dream-vision. In his left hand, he holds the Pharao's cup. Surrounding him is a grape vine, with clusters ready for harvesting. By focusing on the numerological implications of "three days" (the length of the cup bearer's imprisonment), the commentary dwells on the Paschal triduum and the mystery enacted in that period of time.

Thus, the cup bearer locked in the stocks parallels Christ fastened to the cross. The clusters of grapes represent the blood of Jesus shed in the winepress of the cross, action that is commemorated and reenacted sacramentally and liturgically. The cup in the illustration signifies the sacred vessel in which the wine becomes the blood of Jesus. The commentary focuses on the events of Good Friday, Holy Saturday, and Easter Sunday. Redemption occurs at the bloody sacrifice of the crucifixion; the liberation from captivity occurs with the descent into, and harrowing of hell, associated with Holy Saturday. That liberation culminates on Easter Sunday, when

Christ emerges from the darkness and confinement of the tomb and promises similar deliverance from Satan, sin, and death to those who are redeemed.

Figure 31. The rod of Aaron flowers unnaturally by divine power

Numbers 17–18, the basis of this illustration and commentary, describes how God established a process for the selection of priests for the sanctuary. He instructed Moses to gather one staff from each ancestral house — 12 in all — and to place them in the meeting tent in front of the commandments. When on the next day Moses entered the tent, the rod of his brother, Aaron, of the ancestral house of Levi had sprouted shoots, blossoms, and almonds, a sign that the Lord favored him and his family for the priesthood. Pursuing analogies, the commentary contends that Aaron's rod and the Virgin Mary both germinated contrary to the laws of nature and because of divine intervention. That is, the staff grew, and Mary conceived miraculously. Furthermore, the almonds on Aaron's staff are likened to Jesus. Inside the shell of the nuts is the sweet meat, and hidden behind the human nature and form of Jesus is his divinity. The illustration and commentary stress bounty and plenitude, using images of growth and fertility to suggest the magnitude and magnanimity of God's grace. Aaron's flowering rod as a sign of divine approval anticipates a legend in the apocryphal gospels concerning Joseph. In selecting Mary's spouse, the Lord chose a similar method to manifest approval. Among the staffs of the candidates, he permitted Joseph's to flower. Aaron's flowering rod as a sign of fertility parallels the imagery of the Tree of Jesse, wherein the rod, signifying the Virgin Mary, bears the flower, which represents Christ. And, finally, the flowering rod of Aaron identifying the priesthood prefigures iconography of the cross with blossoms and even fruit, whereon Christ is both priest and sacrifice. That fruit and its juice, when sacramentally administered, are available in their bounty and plenitude to all humankind.

Figure 32. The sibyl sees a virgin with a child

In *Legenda Aurea* or *Golden Legend* (see Voragine, 1, 27), the basis appears for figure 32's illustration and commentary. Ruling, in effect, over the entire known world, Caesar Augustus, revered by his subjects as a quasi-divinity, consulted the sibyl to learn whether there would be a ruler greater than himself. The illustration shows the sibyl and Augustus beholding a vision of the Virgin Mary and Christ child who appeared brightly illuminated in the heavens. This vision occurred in Rome on the very day of Christ's nativity in Judea. Fearing the greatness of this child, and the power of God under whose aegis this sovereign was born, Augustus forbade disclosure and invocation of the Lord. The illustration shows Augustus, his hands extended after he had laid aside his scepter, which is on the ground. Kneeling, he glances heavenward in an attitude of fear, awe, and wonder. His attitude is similar to that of homage, which is partially manifested because he relinquishes only his scepter. He has not doffed his crown, a sign that he still clings to his own sovereignty.

Augustus, like other worldly sovereigns, judges greatness by the expanse and duration of sovereignty and the number of one's subjects. On all fronts, however, even imperial Rome and all earthly realms thereafter must yield to the kingdom of Christ, which transcends time and place. Or, to put it differently, the kingdom of Christ is in the afterlife, an eternal realm whose subjects include all humankind. In several ways, the fear of Augustus may be likened to that of Herod, king of Judea, who feels threatened by the newly born Jesus. The slaying of Christians in the early Roman Empire and the Massacre of the Innocents under Herod are ways by which insecure worldly sovereigns manifest their fear. On the other hand, the Magi, presumably kings from the Middle East or Asia Minor, pay true homage to the Christ child.

Chapter 9

Figure 33. The three Magi with gifts adore the child

From Matthew 2.1–12, this illustration focuses on the Magi visiting the Christ child. Visible in the firmament is the star of Bethlehem, and in the background is a stable. The Virgin Mary, with the Christ child on her knee, sits at the end of a *chaise longue*. One of the three Magi, having doffed his crown and placed it on the ground, kneels at the feet of the Virgin and child. In doing so, he presents a gift by opening the container in which it is kept. The other two Magi stand while holding their respective gifts and awaiting their turn to pay homage to the child. Unlike Caesar Augustus who also saw a heavenly sign, the Magi subordinate their kingship to that of the newly born Christ. Because they are from faraway lands, and will return there after their encounter with the Lord, they signify the universalism of Christianity and its gradual movement from Bethlehem to the farthest regions and the most diverse cultures of the world. As such, they anticipate the eventual role of the disciples, who at the very end of Matthew's Gospel are enjoined by Jesus to go to all nations and to make disciples by baptizing and teaching them the Christian message.

Appropriately, the commentary cites and explains an Old Testament prefiguration of the Magi's bravery in traveling to Judea. David's three soldiers traveled bravely into the camp of their enemies, the Philistines, at Bethlehem, acquired water from a cistern, and brought it back to their king (2 Kings 23.15–17). The commentary then characterizes the Magi's visit to Bethlehem as a quest for "the water of eternal grace." Finally, the cistern at Bethlehem from which David's soldiers drew water foreshadows "that the heavenly cup bearer would be born there."

Figure 34. The three Magi see a new star in the East

Also from Matthew 2.1–12, the illustration and commentary treat the journey of the Magi who were guided by the star. Mounted on horses, one of which also has certain features of a camel (the neck, head, and face), the Magi travel in the direction highlighted by the star overhead. The commentary asserts that the coming of the Magi prefigures the conversion of the pagans. If such is true for the people of Asia Minor, it also holds for the Romans who were converted to Christianity in the early years of the apostolic ministry. And, of course, the Roman emperor Constantine himself was converted to Christianity in the early fourth century. The commentary likens the Christ child to Solomon as a babe, who despite his youth was wise. The commentary also likens the adult Solomon at the height of his splendor to Christ. The Old Testament personage triumphed over his adversaries and constructed a stately palace and a magnificent temple. Solomon thus prefigures Christ the King in his role as *Christus Victor* in his glorification and exaltation at the Resurrection, the Ascension, and the Second Coming. As Scripture forecasts, he will come again in "power and glory," and when enthroned on high, he will oversee the Final Judgment. Because Solomon's reputation as a veritable "king of kings" was widespread, he elicited the admiration of other rulers, who visited with him to view the splendor of his kingdom. They also presented him with gifts. Notable among the visitors was the Queen of Saba, whose visit of homage to Solomon elicited her extraordinary praise: that the reports of his splendorous kingdom had fallen short of what she actually witnessed (3 Kings 10.1–13). By her gifts, the Queen of Saba foreshadows the visitation of the Magi with the gold, incense, and myrrh that they presented to the Christ child.

Figure 35. Three soldiers bring water to King David from a cistern

Three soldiers bring water to King David, as recounted in 2 Kings 23.15–17. In the illustration, David props a scepter in the crook of his left arm. His right arm is parallel to the floor, but the right hand is elevated upward, palm outward, the gesture by which he declines the water. One of the soldiers, kneeling on his left knee, presents the water in a pitcher to King David. The attitude of the soldier resembles that of the Magi before the Christ child. By declining the water, and offering it, instead, to the Lord, David prefigures the Virgin Mary, who in giving birth to the Christ child yields him back to the Lord to fulfill the sacrificial ministry of redemption. While the present commentary focuses on the grandeur of Solomon's throne, the illustration depicts David on his modest thronelet. By highlighting the progression from David to Solomon, who overcame his adversaries, enlarged the realm, and constructed a stately palace and magnificent temple, the commentary uses a worldly kingdom under the aegis of the Lord to signify the ineffable eternal kingdom. Accordingly, the commentary parallels Solomon enthroned, the principal emblem of his resplendent kingdom, to the majesty of the Virgin Mary.

The throne — the materials of its construction and their colors, as well as its elevation — represents allegorically the constellation of the Virgin Mary's virtues and her lofty status hierarchically, for she surpasses all those who are deemed blessed on earth. The 12 lions at the sides of the steps that lead to the dais and throne signify the apostles who attend to the Virgin Mary, accompaniment suggested, for instance, in accounts in Acts of the Apostles (1.14). Not to be discounted is the possibility that the lions signify the tribe of Judah, from which the Virgin Mary was descended. After all, Jacob described his son Judah as "a lion recumbent, the king of beasts," and from him "the scepter shall never depart" (Genesis 49.9–10).

Figure 36. The throne of Solomon

Continuing to elaborate on the throne of Solomon, which is actually featured in this next illustration, the commentary suggests that the 12 lions designate the ancestors of Mary, presumably the patriarchs from whom she descended, including Judah. The commentary likens the larger lions flanking Solomon enthroned to "the two tablets of the law that Mary holds fast within her heart and power." While the decalogue inscribed in stone comes to mind, more apt, however, is the New Testament counterpart — the two great commandments written on the tablets of flesh in the heart (2 Corinthians 3.3). As such, Mary is the principal exemplar and embodiment of the New Covenant. The commentary refers to the round ceiling above Solomon's throne as an image of the perfection of Mary, who "is immaculate without any untidy corners." Though the commentary, which refers to the illustration, cites two "hands [that] hold up the throne on both sides" — the one representing the Father, the other, the Holy Spirit — these details are not pictured. Nevertheless, the commentary asserts that these Divine Persons are ever-present with the Virgin Mary.

Hearkening back to the three Magi — and, by implication, to the journey of the Queen of Saba to Solomon's court — the commentary dwells on the significance of the three gifts. Gold, frankincense, and myrrh typify the respective roles of Jesus as king, priest, and sacrificial offering. The commentary explicitly or implicitly indicates that Jesus enacts all three roles at the crucifixion. He is royal as Christ the King when enthroned on the cross; he is sacerdotal while he presides at the altar of the cross; and he is sacrificial in offering himself as the victim in the New Dispensation. The commentary also correlates the gifts with humankind's devout responses to the three roles of Jesus: the gold of love for the king's submission to suffering, the frankincense of praise and thanksgiving for his priesthood, and the myrrh as a sign of compassion for, and remembrance of, his death. Significantly, in preparing the body of Jesus for burial, Nicodemus uses myrrh, an aromatic gum resin (John 19.39–40), and the three women who visit the tomb presumably included myrrh among the spices and unguents that they carried to anoint the body of Jesus.

Chapter 10

Figure 37. Mary presents her son in the temple

From Luke 2.22–39, figure 37 centers upon two interrelated events — the Presentation of the infant Jesus in the temple and the Purification of the Virgin Mary. Devout Jews consecrated their first-born sons to the Lord (Exodus 13.2,12). The woman who had given birth to a boy was declared unclean, but she underwent a process of cleansing that culminated on the fortieth day after childbirth: With a year-old lamb and a turtledove or pigeon — or a pair of turtle-doves and two young pigeons, without a lamb — the woman visited a priest, who sacrificed them on her behalf (Leviticus 12.2–8). In the illustration, the priest appears at the one side of the altar, atop which the Christ child stands. At the other side is Mary, but Joseph does not appear. In the account of the Presentation and the Purifi-cation, Luke's Gospel highlights the involvement of Simeon and Anna, who were awaiting the restoration of the Lord's rule in Israel through the Messiah. At the temple when the Christ child was pre-sented to the Lord, Simeon and Anna both testify that he is the Messiah who will fulfill the expectations of the people. At times, these two figures — Simeon without Anna, or she without him — appear in illustrations of the Presentation and the Purification. Neither one appears in the present illustration, which shows two other women in Mary's company. The one woman appears to carry a container, presumably with the fledglings, either two turtledoves or two pigeons, to be sacrificed on Mary's behalf. Though Mary, who is sinless, need not be purified, she complies with the law as stipu-lated in Leviticus. Perhaps the three women, including Mary, in the illustration of the Presentation anticipate the visit by the three women to the tomb of Jesus (Luke 24.1–12). If so, then the three women who witness the Christ child being presented to the Lord have as their counterparts the three women who witness his death, the consummation of his service to the Lord.

Figure 38. The Ark of the Covenant signifies Mary

In Exodus 25.10–22, the Lord specifies the construction of the Ark of the Covenant. This commentary likens the ark to the Virgin Mary, the former containing the law on stone tablets and the latter observing them from within herself. While the commentary glosses each of the commandments, all ten may be subsumed under the two great commandments of the New Dispensation (Matthew 22.37–40). That is, the first four commandments deal with one's love of God, the next six with love of one's neighbor. Traditionally, it is believed that the first four commandments were on the one tablet, and the remaining six on the other. And while the fourth commandment, which requires obedience to one's mother and father, seems not to relate to God, it does entrust to parents a certain authority for the righteous upbringing of their children. In this matter, parents are accountable to the Lord.

The commentary continues to liken various details of the ark — both materials and construction — to the Virgin Mary. The ark houses the law, which Mary read in Scripture; Aaron's staff blossomed at the ark (Numbers 17.18–20), and Mary is the branch that bore a flower and fruit; the ark includes a golden urn with manna, so too Mary houses Jesus, the bread of life; the wood of the ark did not decay, and Mary remains incorruptible, spiritually but also physically. That is, it is believed that Mary's death was akin to sleep, hence a dormition, so that she never suffered decomposition, and at her Assumption was taken whole and intact heavenward. Though the commentary refers to the four rings of gold on the ark, the illustration lacks these crucial devices. God specified that four rings were to be fastened to the ark — two on the one side, and two on the opposite side. Through these rings, two poles were placed for transporting the ark (Exodus 25.12–16). The commentary likens the four rings to the cardinal virtues of Mary.

Figure 39. The candelabrum of Solomon's temple

Exodus 25.31–40 furnishes the biblical context for the next illustration and commentary, which center on the lampstand in Solomon's temple. The four feet on which the lampstand rests, perhaps, may be correlated with the cardinal virtues that the Virgin Mary exemplifies: "temperance, prudence, fortitude, and justice, the roots and the beginning of all the other virtues." The commentary recalls the two poles by which the ark is transported, likening them to "the double nature of love found in Mary, love of God and love of neighbor." In this way, the commentary affirms Mary's observance of the two great commandments of the New Dispensation. The seven branches of the lampstand are correlated with the corporal works of mercy (Matthew 25.35–39), which Mary also embodies, the works that issue from the two great commandments and the cardinal virtues, not to mention the Beatitudes (Matthew 5.3–11).

The dominant imagery of the illustration and commentary is that of light, which is applied in myriad ways to the Virgin Mary. She becomes "the candlestick kindled by divine fire" and the "lamp lit by the divine light." Furthermore, the commentary cites luminaries in the firmament — the sun, moon, and stars — as metaphors of the Virgin Mary's effulgence. In doing so, the implication is that the luminaries in the heavens were created by God as sources of light at the first Creation; like them, Mary was kindled by God as a source of light, though on the earth itself not in the remote firmament. The proximity of that light and its presence in Mary evoke wonder, awe, and admiration, so that she becomes, in effect, the cynosure of the gazes of humankind. To describe her, moreover, as "the light of the angels" suggests her lofty position even with reference to purely spiritual beings. Her unique status as the mother of Jesus, the light-bringer, is celebrated among the various titles by which she is invoked, including Queen of the Angels, in the litanies extolling her.

Figure 40. The boy Samuel is offered to the Lord

From 1 Kings 1.5–28, the illustration features, at the right, the mother of Samuel, Anna, presenting him to the Lord in the temple.

Behind her are her husband, Elcana, and perhaps Peninna, his other wife at the time. Whereas he had several children by Peninna, he had none by Anna, who was barren. In praying to the Lord that she might conceive a son, Anna promised that if her wish were granted, she would present the child for a lifetime of service to the Lord. In the illustration, the priest Eli receives the child Samuel from Anna. The commentary aligns several events in the lives of Samuel and Jesus, some of them issuing from the actions of their mothers (respectively Anna and the Virgin Mary). In the illustration, Anna holds a lit taper. Though it, as such, is not identified in the commentary, it presumably underlies the imagery of light and sacrifice that characterizes the comparison of Samuel and Jesus. This imagery bears directly on the Presentation of Jesus, who is recognized by Simeon as the Messiah and "the light of revelation," which the commentary recounts in its paraphrase of Luke 2.32. While the commentary does not cite Old Testament analogues for such imagery of light, clearcut examples occur in the prophetic utterances of Isaias. Prophesying the recognition of, and reaction to, the Messiah, Isaias contends that the "people who have walked in darkness have seen a great light" and on "these who dwelt in a land of gloom a light has shone" (Isaias 9.1–2). In effect, Simeon echoes these and other Old Testament prophecies in order to announce their fulfillment in the coming of Jesus. The commentary also cites Simeon's statement to the Virgin Mary: that a sword will pierce her heart (Luke 2.35), a reference to the grief that she will experience in witnessing the suffering and death of her son.

Chapter 11

Figure 41. All the idols fall to the ground when Jesus enters Egypt

Three biblical texts — one from the New Testament, and two from the Old — constitute the frame of reference for this illustration and commentary, which concentrate on the flight of the Holy Family into Egypt, the means to escape the threat of King Herod to the Christ child. The account in Matthew 2.13–18 provides the most details of the journey. In the illustration, Mary and the Christ child sit on a donkey, while Joseph on foot leads the way. Across his left shoulder, Joseph carries a walking stick, from which a bag is suspended. As such, Joseph anticipates the later travel of Jesus along the *via dolorosa*. There, Jesus at his Passion will carry the cross, which leans against his left shoulder. The other two biblical texts provide the basis for the image at the left of the illustration, the toppling of the Egyptian idols from their pedestal as the Christ child passes by. In Isaias 19. 1, the prophecy — ". . . the Lord is riding on a swift cloud on his way to Egypt; the idols of Egypt tremble before him" — elicits visual representation through the flight into Egypt, the only actual presence of Jesus in that realm. And in Jeremias 43.11–13, the Lord foresees that King Nabuchodonosor of Babylon "shall set fire to the temples of Egypt's gods, and burn the gods or carry them off"; "he shall smash the obelisks of the temple of the sun in the land of Egypt. . . ." The commentary, however, by drawing on the apocryphal gospels and other legends concerning the Christ child in Egypt, material compiled in Peter Comestor's *Historia Scholastica* (*PL*, CXCVIII, 1543), is extra-scriptural in developing the role of Jeremias as a prophet. Though indeed Jeremias was in Egypt, nothing is known of his stay there; nevertheless, the commentary characterizes him as prophesying to the Egyptians that a child born of a maiden will cause the statues of their gods to topple. When Christ enters Egypt, the prophecy is fulfilled.

Figure 42. The Egyptians make a statue of a virgin with an infant

Figure 42 continues to stress the Christ child in Egypt, not to mention his effect on the Egyptian idols. The illustration features a statue of the Virgin Mary and the Christ child enthroned, which the Egyptians created after Jeremias prophesied the toppling of the Egyptian idols. Accepting that prophecy, some Egyptians recognized the power and preeminence of the child over their gods, thereafter carving a statue in his honor while awaiting his arrival and its consequences. Additionally, the commentary cites an Old Testament personage, notably Moses, who prefigures the presence of the Christ child in Egypt. These interrelated accounts of the Christ child and of Moses derive from apocryphal and legendary sources, materials compiled, among other places, in Peter Comestor's *Historia Scholastica* (*PL*, CXCVIII, 1142–1144, 1440, 1543). With these same apocryphal and legendary sources, the commentary then intersperses reference to Scripture. In Exodus 1.8–22, the Pharao, fearful that the Hebrews who were growing in numbers and strength might pose a threat to the Egyptians, ordered the drowning in the river of newly born Hebrew males.

The commentary names the parents of Moses, though Scripture (Exodus 2.1) identifies them only as Levites. The commentary reflects the wish of Moses' parents to live separately, so that the wife would not conceive; but a sign from God persuaded them to do otherwise. Then the commentary echoes Scripture (Exodus 2.2–10): how, to save her child, the mother of Moses placed him in a basket at the river, where the Pharao's daughter found and eventually adopted him. Rounding off the commentary is the extra-scriptural account of Moses breaking the Pharao's crown, on which appeared an image of the Egyptian god Amon; the ensuing suspicion that Moses is the realization of the Hebrew threat against the Egyptians; and the consumption of coals by Moses as a sign that he is a foolish boy, not a serious menace.

Figure 43. Moses throws down the Pharao's crown and shatters it

Illustrated here is the disintegration of the Pharao's crown by the boy Moses. The commentary then interrelates this extra-scriptural episode with episodes involving the Christ child in Egypt. Just as Moses, in order to lead the Hebrews out of Egypt, was saved by God from the Pharao's edict of doom — that all male children of the Jews should be drowned — so also Christ escapes the massacre of the Innocents ordered by King Herod. The shattering of Pharao's crown with the image of the god Amon parallels the toppling of the Egyptian idols when the Christ child entered Egypt. The Pharao as a political potentate ruled under the aegis of the gods of Egypt, and the kings of Israel did likewise under Yahweh. Against these temporal and worldly kingdoms, which are in a constant state of conflict with one another and within themselves, the commentary provides a mystical interpretation of Jesus as liberator: he frees humankind from Hell. The church fathers typically associate Egypt with Hell, the Pharao with Satan, and the Egyptian crocodile with Leviathan. Leviathan with its enormous jaws and teeth conventionally represents the mouth and jaws of Hell. Exiting Egypt, the Christ child anticipates his later role in the harrowing of Hell, whereby he leads from captivity the patriarchs, prophets, and kings of the Old Dispensation. Having conquered the domain of Satan, where at times he shatters the gates (in iconography of the harrowing of Hell), Jesus typically leads the multitude of his redeemed to his eternal realm, which supersedes time and place, and for which the appellation "Christ the King" is supernaturally meaningful. While metaphors of military and political power explain Christ's conquest, the irony is that his sovereignty is radically different from its figurative representation. Finally, Christ himself forecasts his Second Coming in "power and glory" (Mark 13.24–27, Matthew 16.27–28), when he will be enthroned as both King and Judge.

Figure 44. Nabuchodonosor sees a large statue in a dream

From Daniel 2.1–49, this illustration and commentary center upon Nabuchodonosor's dream, some details of which are provided in the commentary on Figure 44. The dream envisions a statue, the parts of its body composed of various metals, though its feet are made partially of clay. In the dream, a huge stone, hewn from a mountain without human intervention, crushed the statue. When Nabuchodonosor requests an interpretation of his dream, his countrymen profess inability to do so. Daniel, however, interprets the dream for the king, at first emphasizing its political implications for the future: each of the various metals making up the statue represents a different kingdom in the ebb and flow of history, one giving way to another, and so forth.

Daniel's interpretation ends with an analysis of the large stone and its destructive effect on the statue: "In the lifetime of those kings the God of heaven will set up a kingdom that shall never be destroyed or delivered up to another people; rather, it shall break in pieces all these kingdoms and put an end to them, and it shall stand forever" (Daniel 2.44). The commentary, in effect, elaborates on this scriptural interpretation, at times resorting to apocrypha and legends, most notably in likening the disintegration of the statue in Nabuchodonosor's dream to the toppling of the idols when Christ entered Egypt. Further elaboration in the commentary likewise dwells on the Christic significance of the dream. The stone that is hewn without human intervention signifies Jesus who "is born of Mary without human assistance." Just as the stone grew in size, so too does faith in Jesus, which results in the destruction of idolatry. The increasing size of the stone diminishes by contrast the enemies of Jesus, who "are almost reduced to nothing." The mountain represents the growth of Jesus — from infancy and adolescence to adulthood — in age and wisdom, until he fills creation. The humankind of "clean hands" and "pure heart" who ascend that mountain — after the manner of ascents to mountaintops in the Old Testament — will see the Lord, gain salvation, and enjoy their view of him eternally.

Chapter 12

Figure 45. John baptizes Jesus in the Jordan

The first event of the public ministry of Jesus, his baptism in the Jordan, occurred when he was approximately 30 years old (John 1.29–34). In the illustration, Jesus, knee-deep in the river, assumes an attitude of prayer; behind his head is a nimbus with a cruciform image. On the one bank is John the Baptizer, kneeling. In his right hand he holds a laver from which he pours water. The water descending onto the head of Jesus forms an arc against the cross emblazoned on the nimbus. As such, the imagery anticipates the issuance of water from Christ crucified, an event considered to be the mystical origin of the sacrament of baptism. At the same time, the arc of the water suggests an outpouring of grace from the heavens, which opened up at the baptism of the Lord. As Scripture recounts, and as the illustration depicts, the Holy Spirit, figured as a dove, appears above Jesus. In this context, then, the arc of baptismal water suggests the cleansing and purgation of the world after the Deluge, at which the appearance of the dove signifies renewed peace between humankind and the godhead (Genesis 8.11–12). Scripture also recounts that the Father affirmed the divinity of Jesus by identifying him as "beloved Son." On the bank opposite John the Baptizer is an angel, who, like Jesus, stands in an attitude of prayer. In contrast to baptism by blood and by fire, the commentary stresses the importance of water. By his immersion in a river, Jesus chose to "impart a power to water." The commentary likewise cites an Old Testament prefiguration of the sacrament of baptism — namely, the account of the bronze sea, or large circular fount with an enormous brim resting on several stands (3 Kings 7.23–39). This was placed at Solomon's temple for the ritualistic purification of priests.

Figure 46. Those entering the temple wash in a bronze laver

From 3 Kings 7.23–39, this illustration and commentary explain the bronze laver and its significance to an understanding of baptism. Because Jesus was baptized in water, it acquires such crucial importance in ritualistic cleansing that other liquids may not be used. Citing the several metals that were used in the construction of the laver, notably bronze, an alloy of copper and tin, and pure copper, the commentary likens this diversity to the multiplicity of languages in which the sacrament of baptism is performed, though the rubrics are uniform. The 12 oxen that face outward from the base of the stand signify the 12 Apostles "who spread baptism throughout the world." The reference presumably is to the enjoinder by Jesus who, at the very end of Matthew's Gospel, commands the apostles to evangelize and baptize disciples in all nations. Though the ox is the symbol of Luke, whose gospel emphasizes the sacrificial ministry of Jesus, in the illustration it pertains to each of the Apostles, appropriately. Each of them, with the exception of John, died in martyrdom while disseminating the newly found faith. The ox was also a principal means of transport and source of power in tilling the fields in the biblical era. As such, it aptly signifies the transmission of the faith by the apostles and its growth under their labor.

The commentary also dwells on the preliminary examination of conscience required for the baptism of adults. Therefore, the mirror above the bronze laver signifies the exercise of self-examination and the acquisition of heightened self-knowledge, leading, in sequence, to a rejection of sinfulness, a penitential state of mind, and a contrite heart. Rounding off the commentary are two scriptural citations, the one from the New Testament, the other from the Old Testament. The first centers on John the Baptizer's rebuke of the Pharisees, who approached him for baptism though their hearts were not contrite. The second recounts the story of Naaman, who was healed of leprosy at the Jordan River.

Figure 47. The leper Naaman [bathes] seven times and is cleansed

Figure 47 issues from 4 Kings 5.1–19, in which Naaman, army commander for the king of Aram, encounters the prophet Eliseus. Afflicted by leprosy, Naaman is advised to bathe seven times in the Jordan River. Doing so, he is healed, so that his skin thereafter resembles an infant's, an image of restored physical health that reflects the spiritual wholeness brought on by baptism. The commentary links the sevenfold immersion in the Jordan River to the removal of the seven deadly sins. The purity that ensues after baptism would enable one, were he to die without having sinned again, to enter directly into the Kingdom of Heaven. Substantiating this view with a reference to the opening of the heavens when Jesus was baptized, the commentary implies that the appearance of the

Holy Spirit as a dove and the Father's vocal affirmation of the divinity of Jesus testify to the efficacy of baptism in providing the grace of salvation. The commentary likewise cites the crossing of the Jordan by the Chosen People and their entrance into the Promised Land as a prefiguration of the efficacy of Baptism, a prerequisite for salvation. The relationship cited between the Chosen People who had to cross the Jordan and the requirement "to pass through the baptismal font" was graphically manifested ritualistically in the early church. Baptism was celebrated as part of the Paschal triduum — in particular, at the transition from pre-dawn darkness to first light on Easter Sunday. The catechumens entered a river from the one bank, passed through the water (and for a brief period were totally immersed), and emerged gradually onto the opposite bank. As they emerged, they saw the Easter sunrise, a sign of the heavens opening up to them. Even more graphically, the minister officiating or someone assisting him at the celebration of baptism was on the opposite bank with a cross elevated against the sunrise, an indelible image of salvation.

Figure 48. The Jordan is dry for the crossing of the children of God

From Josue 3.7–17 and 4.1–18, this illustration and commentary highlight how the Chosen People crossed the Jordan under the leadership of Josue. Scripture records that the waters of the Jordan were amassed above the point of the crossing, while the waters below flowed to the sea. The effect was to create a dry crossing for the Chosen People, who proceeded at first behind the ark of the covenant that the priests carried. Midway at the crossing, the scene depicted in the present illustration, the carriers remained stationary until the entire nation passed to the other side, then the ark was transported into the Promised Land. When the carriers stepped onto the bank, the waters of the river began to flow again. Yahweh instructed Josue to choose 12 men, one representative from each of the tribes of Israel. From midway in the Jordan, where the ark of the covenant was stationary, each man was to take up a stone, and all 12 stones were to be transported to the site of the Israelites' camp and to serve thereafter as a memorial of the miraculous crossing. Josue set up 12 stones midway in the Jordan to mark the spot where the feet of the carriers of the ark had rested during the crossing. In the present illustration the stones appear in the dry bed of the Jordan River, though it is uncertain whether they are the ones not yet taken up by the 12 tribesmen or the ones set there by Josue after the tribesmen had performed their duty. What is crucial in the commentary is the numerological significance of the number 12 — the 12 tribes of Israel foreshadow the 12 Apostles. The former crossed the Jordan into the Promised Land, the latter in evangelizing and baptizing afforded the opportunity of salvation to the peoples of many nations. The commentary also focuses on the ark of the covenant, the materials of its construction and the sacred objects contained in it, and expounds their Christological significance.

Chapter 13

Figure 49. Christ is tempted by the devil in three different ways

From Matthew 4.1–10, the illustration and commentary center upon the temptation of Jesus in the wilderness, which occurs right after his baptism in the Jordan River. The Holy Spirit, having appeared as a dove overhead during the baptism of Jesus, impels or inspires him to travel to the desert. There, he is subject to adversity, including hunger because of a 40-day fast. The devil, sensing the vulnerability of Jesus, tempts him. He does so by appearing as a man who uses persuasive arguments to advance each of three temptations. Though the commentary stresses the appearance of the tempter as a man, the illustration shows him as a demon to indicate that Jesus was able to penetrate the pretense of evil-fair-seeming and discern the treachery of his adversary. The illustration depicts the first temptation, when the devil, with stones in his hands, requests that Jesus turn them into bread. On the stomach of the devil is the face and head of a man, which signify that the higher rational nature of humankind has been degraded, so much so that it is portrayed at the place in the human body associated with appetites. The effect of such degradation permits upstart passions or appetites to gain ascendance over the natural and legitimate preeminence of reason in humankind. Tempting Jesus to relinquish rational self-control, the devil is thwarted. Jesus contends that the bread of life is really the word of God. The commentary stresses the persistence of the devil, who launches another temptation if previous ones fail. Permitting himself to be tempted, the Son by his experiences and his triumphs exemplifies to all humankind that temptation is inevitable, but it can be overcome by assistance from God.

Figure 50. Daniel destroys Bel and kills the dragon

The illustration portrays an episode from Daniel 14.1–27, involving Daniel's slaying of the dragon and the destruction of the Babylonian idol Bel, though the commentary continues to explicate the significance of the temptations in the wilderness. By likening the countless demons to specks of dust visible in the rays of the sun, the commentary emphasizes the various temptations that beset humankind. Of the three major temptations directed at Christ — gluttony, pride, avarice — the commentary elaborates on the first, by comparing Christ's hunger to that of Adam and Eve who yielded to gluttony and did partake of the forbidden fruit. The commentary implies thereby that the tempter opportunely accosted Adam and Eve when they were hungry, a condition that made them more susceptible to his approach; the tempter in the wilderness appraised Christ as he fasted to be more vulnerable to seduction. Though the commentary is silent about the parallelism between Christ's temptations in the wilderness and the adversities of the Chosen People, the hunger suffered by the Israelites caused them to murmur against God, who provided them with manna. Whereas the Chosen People yielded to their physical hunger, Jesus resisted the onset of appetite. The second temptation, that of pride, afflicts the Israelites who presumptuously expect that the Lord will protect them, his Chosen People, from danger in the wilderness. The Lord, therefore, is often put to the test by the Israelites, who petition him expectantly for miraculous intervention on their behalf. Jesus, in resisting the devil's temptation that he jeopardize his safety in order to elicit rescue by divine intervention, knows that one does not request miracles as a sign of God's Providential care for humankind. Finally, the temptation of avarice besets the Israelites when they build a worldly kingdom and expand it by conquest, whereas Jesus in the wilderness rejects the devil's offer of numerous worldly kingdoms, for he knows that the only truly durable realm and sovereignty are in the afterlife.

Figure 51. David overcomes Goliath, the Philistine

While this illustration depicts David's slaying of Goliath from 1 Kings 17.23–51, the commentary continues to focus on the gluttony and immoderation that Jesus resists in the temptations in the wilderness and their prefiguration by Daniel's triumphs over the idol Bel and of the dragon that dwelled in a cave nearby. Daily the idol, presumed to be a living god, was presented with large amounts of food and drink, but secretly the priests, their wives, and children entered the temple to eat and drink what was there. When Daniel exposed their ruse to the king, he had the priests, their wives, and children all slain; and Daniel by the king's permission destroyed the idol Bel and the temple. Nearby, however, dwelled a dragon, whom the Babylonians also worshiped as a living god, but Daniel claimed that he could kill it without sword or club. Receiving the king's approval to do so, Daniel boiled together pitch, grease, and hair into cakes like balls, which the dragon consumed. And then the dragon disintegrated. In the illustration Daniel holds the dragon at bay with a sword while six balls are shown on the table, and the seventh is held by the king's fool or jester. The king, wearing a crown and holding a scepter, stands nearby.

While the commentary does not explicate the numerological significance of the seven balls, it seems likely that they refer to the deadly sins, among them gluttony, which brings on the downfall of the priests of Bel, along with their wives and children, and of the dragon. Rounding off the commentary is brief reference to David's slaying of Goliath, whose pride is another example of a deadly sin that Jesus resisted in the wilderness.

Figure 52. David kills a bear and a lion

While the illustration here depicts David overcoming a bear and a lion (1 Kings 17.34–37), the commentary continues to explicate the significance of the youth's slaying of Goliath. When Jesse, the father of David, instructed his young son to visit his three older brothers at their camp and to bring them foodstuffs, he overheard the taunts and challenges of Goliath. David bristled at the insults and spoke his mind to his brothers and the other Israelites. King Saul summoned David, who volunteered to engage Goliath; and as evidence of his courage he reports that in tending his father's sheep, he has singlehandedly slain a bear and a lion that were preying on the flock. The commentary likens Goliath's pride, a deadly sin, to that of Lucifer, and David is celebrated for his humility, manifested in reliance on the living God who infused him with strength. David, therefore, prefigures the humility of Jesus, the virtuous antidote to the second temptation, that of pride. In explaining the temptation of pride, the commentary cites its various manifestations, especially vainglory and the desire to be praised. The vice is so insidious that it may be found in many places, ranging from kingship, on the one hand, to life in the cloister, on the other. The commentary also glosses the significance of David's slaying of the bear and lion. As predators, both animals are symbols of avarice. In protecting the sheep and in killing the predators, David in effect triumphs over avarice, thereby foreshadowing the triumph of Jesus over the third temptation in the wilderness and, finally, over his tempter.

Chapter 14

Figure 53. Magdalen repents in the house of Simon

From Luke 7.36–50, we find here the penitential woman who visits Jesus in the home of Simon, the Pharisee. Traditionally, interpreters have identified the woman as Mary Magdalen, largely because of Luke 8.2, which recounts that Jesus expelled seven demons from her, presumably the capital sins. In the illustration, the penitential woman is on her knees at the feet of Christ. She bathes his feet with her tears, wipes his feet dry with her hair, kisses, and applies ointment to them. As the commentary indicates, Jesus, after his own baptism in the Jordan River and his temptation in the wilderness, began to preach repentance and to forecast Doomsday. At his baptism, onlookers witnessed the opening of the kingdom of heaven, and thereafter Jesus stressed its accessibility to penitents who strive to receive the Lord's merciful forgiveness. A case in point is the penitential woman or Mary Magdalen, who presumably heeded the preaching of Jesus and sought forgiveness. At Simon's home, she manifests her penitential state and profound humility, not to mention gratitude for the opportunity to be forgiven. Her very manner constitutes a petition for forgiveness and an expression of thanksgiving. The commentary explains, metaphorically, that the sinner incurs indebtedness, but he or she is released from financial obligation by forgiveness. Significantly, the conversation of Jesus with Simon deals with a creditor who forgives two debtors, one of whom owes ten times more than the other. Jesus questions Simon concerning which debtor will love the creditor more. Simon replies, and Jesus concurs, that the debtor who owed more will have greater love. In posing such a question, Jesus is explaining that Mary Magdalen's graphic conduct reflects the depth of her love, for her indebtedness as an egregious sinner, known even to Simon, was most substantial.

Figure 54. Manasses does penance in captivity

This illustration and commentary commingle three passages — the one from 2 Kings 21.1–18, the other from 2 Chronicles 33.1–20, and a third, 2 Paralipomenon 33.1–19 (see *The Apocrypha and Pseudo-epigraphia of the Old Testament in English*, ed. R. H. Charles [Oxford, 1913], I, 62–624). In the illustration, King Manasses appears in the stocks, after God has delivered him to his enemies, the Assyrians. For decades, King Manasses had practiced impieties against God, at times even defiling the places of worship to the Lord by erecting in them altars to false gods. Having been captured by the Assyrians and transported to Babylon, the king undergoes a conversion (2 Chronicles 33.11–12), for which he serves as a prototype of the egregious sinner who is reformed. The commentary emphasizes the stages of the conversion of Manasses: he acknowledges his sinfulness, manifests contrition, sheds copious tears of lamentation, professes unworthiness to be saved, affirms the justness of God's wrath, and praises the bounty of God's mercy. The commentary upholds Manasses as a hopeful model for all sinners, but especially grievous ones whose sins are classified as mortal but whose conversion is nevertheless possible. If, however, a sinner perseveres in obduracy and becomes, in effect, reprobate, he in effect condemns himself or herself to remain, as the commentary indicates, "a prisoner of the devil." In line with this viewpoint, the illustration of Manasses shows how he, a veritable captive of the devil, has been imprisoned by his sinfulness. But the conversion with the assistance of God brings about a release from imprisonment.

Figure 55. The father and master of the house welcomes the prodigal son

From Luke 15.11–32, the illustration and commentary treat the parable of the prodigal son. In the illustration the prodigal son kneels before his father. He acknowledges that he has sinned not only against his father but also against God. The forgiving father instructs a servant to bring the finest robe, a ring, and shoes — all for the son at his homecoming. In the illustration the servant stands at the extreme right, bearing the accouterments with which the son is to be invested. At the extreme left is the older son, who is disgruntled by the festive welcome that his father has afforded the younger son, a welcome that includes the slaying of the fattest calf. Of the three major characters in the parable — the father, the older son, and the younger one — the commentary stresses the sinfulness and regeneration of the third, with little attention to the first two. This emphasis highlights the interrelation of the Lord's mercy and the prodigal son's repentance, the former promoting and supporting the latter. The prodigal son, moreover, becomes an example of the wayward person who, as the commentary states, "turns away from his heavenly home when he sins." Though St. Augustine's explanation of the source of evil is not cited — a perversion (or turning away and deviation) of the will from goodness — it nevertheless underlies the explanation of sinfulness in the commentary. The sinner, as well, falls into the service of Lucifer, signified by the townsman. Feeding the swine of the townsman, an action likened to feeding one's own devils (or sinful appetites) by sinfulness, the sinner finally becomes spiritually impoverished. At the nadir of his poverty and in the depth of servitude to the devil, the sinner, while eating the very husks that he feeds the animals, comes to experience God's mercy and, because of it, begins the process of recovery and regeneration.

Figure 56. Admonished for adultery, David repents

While this illustration and some of the commentary are based on 2 Kings 12.1–13, the commentary continues to gloss the parable of the prodigal son, stressing that penance is but one means through which the Lord will reclaim a sinner. Penance is likened to flagellation, for the Lord permits the sinner to suffer as a means of just punishment but also as a way to repentance. The Lord, in effect, mercifully provides grace during the suffering of the sinner, assisting to rectify the perverted will and to realign it toward a heavenly orientation. If such occurred with the prodigal son, essentially the

same is true with King David. When Nathan, sent by the Lord, rebukes David for sinfulness, the king acknowledges his misdeeds and
repents. First, David impregnated the wife of Urias. Second, he ordered a military commander to assign Urias to frontline battle,
during which David's men would withdraw, so that the single warrior left behind would be slain by the enemy. Though God forgives
David, he still exacts just punishment for the king's grievous sins,
including the death by illness of the child that David sinfully pro-
created. Thereafter, David and his wife, the widow of Urias, pro-
created another son, who was named Solomon and who of course
prospered. The commentary becomes virtually rhapsodic in its celebration, almost hymnal in tone, of the Lord's mercy, forgiveness,
and love. A catalog of sinners, from the Old and New Testaments,
provides ample evidence that the Lord encourages repentance despite the magnitude and depth of one's sinfulness. Though not explicitly stated, the implication of the commentary is that an unre-
pentant sinner is one who rejects the many opportunities that the
Lord provides for regeneration.

Chapter 15

Figure 57. Christ weeps over the city of Jerusalem

The illustration and commentary derive from Luke 19.28–48, which
recounts Christ's entry into Jerusalem, his lament for that city, and
the driving of the merchants from the temple. He instructed two of
his disciples to acquire a colt for him; they draped their cloaks over
it, and assisted him in mounting it. Praised by the populace who
lined the roadway, spread their cloaks before him, and strewed his
way with palm branches, Jesus rode triumphantly into Jerusalem,
as the illustration dramatizes. The illustration also shows a man in
a tree, waving a branch as Jesus passes by. While one may contend
that this spectator is simply part of the crowd, the illustrator may
be incorporating the story of Zacchaeus (from Luke 18.1–10). Short
of stature, Zacchaeus, a wealthy tax collector, wished to see Jesus.

To do so, he scaled a sycamore tree from which he viewed Jesus, who summoned Zacchaeus to come to him and indicated that he would spend the night at his home. While onlookers murmured that Zacchaeus was a sinner, the tax collector affirmed to Jesus that he gives half of his belongings to the poor; and if he defrauded anyone, he pays him back fourfold.

The commentary also recalls two other events on Palm Sunday: the lament over Jerusalem and the expulsion of the merchants from the temple. First, Jesus weeps over Jerusalem, presumably in anticipation of its destruction in 70 A.D. by the Romans. This razing of Jerusalem signifies the eternal punishment that Jesus foresees for the inhabitants of a city that, despite their present welcome of him, ultimately will reject his messianic message, the very message accepted by Zacchaeus. Second, Jesus, in expelling the merchants from the temple, lays claim to it as a place at which he would preach daily. The merchants guided by monetary self-interest are contrasted with Zacchaeus, whose charitable conduct emanates from his response to the message of Jesus.

Figure 58. Jeremias laments over Jerusalem

Though figure 58 shows Jeremias lamenting over the destruction of Jerusalem (Lamentations 1–2), the commentary does not elaborate on that topic. While this Old Testament prophet prefigures the sorrow of Jesus, the difference is that Jeremias was bemoaning a city already destroyed by the Chaldeans in the sixth century B.C. Jesus foresaw the imminent destruction of Jerusalem by the Romans. The commentary focuses on the praise and honor afforded Jesus by the people of Jerusalem, likening it to the jubilation elicited by David after his triumph over Goliath and to the Israelites' celebration of David's achievements over those of Saul (1 Kings 17.50–58; 18.7). The commentary relates the details of praising and honoring Jesus at Palm Sunday to the process by which humankind expresses gratitude to the Lord for assistance in overcoming sinfulness and in being restored to holiness. The commentary suggests that as a word "Jerusalem" mystically designates a "vision of peace" and spiritually refers to "the truly faithful." The implication is that peace for the faithful will be truly achieved in the Heavenly Jerusalem or Celestial City, and that to prepare to be a participant in that eternal celebration one should always be in a state of readiness, for "the Savior is prepared to come to us at any hour and we, contrite, must hasten to meet Him." The commentary also recognizes the means by which humankind may be restored to holiness or may maintain it: by disciplining the body through self-mortification, by giving to the poor, by performing works of mercy and other virtuous acts, and by praising, honoring, and expressing gratitude to the Lord.

Figure 59. David is welcomed with praise

Drawn from 1 Kings 17.57 and 18.6–9, this recalls the triumphal return of David after he defeated Goliath. David on horseback holds aloft Goliath's head, upright at the end of a pole. Behind David is the army of Israelites, and as he approaches the gates of Jerusalem, men and women emerge to acclaim him and his victory. The commentary, however, deals briefly with the parallelism between Christ's triumphal entrance into Jerusalem and David's. After entering Jerusalem, Jesus will experience the humiliation of the Passion and Crucifixion, so the acclamation by the people proves to be short-lived. Jesus, to be sure, enacts his major triumph during the Paschal triduum, after which the earnest praise, honor, and gratitude bestowed on him by the faithful will contrast with the welcome of the crowd outside Jerusalem. The commentary, on the other hand, focuses on the scourging of the merchants by Jesus in the temple and his overturning of their tables. By implication, however, David's triumph over Goliath results in a rout of the Philistine army, anticipating the wrath of Jesus in dispersing the moneychangers.

But the commentary dwells on another Old Testament prefiguration of the scourging administered by Jesus. From 2 Machabees 3, the account of the beating of Heliodorus tells how this minister of the king of Asia, Seleucus, sought to confiscate wealth for the royal treasury from the temple of Jerusalem. These funds, earmarked for the care of widows and orphans, were much smaller than anticipated, but Heliodorus persisted. At the temple, divine intervention caused panic among the followers of Heliodorus, for a horse and rider appeared. The horse charged Heliodorus, its front hooves thrown against him. Two other men appeared, flogging him to unconsciousness. When he was revived, Heliodorus offered a sacrifice of thanksgiving to the Lord for having spared his life. The implication is that the two young men who flogged Heliodorus prefigure the role of Jesus as the "scourge" of God against the moneychangers.

Figure 60. Heliodorus is scourged

Continuing with the story of Heliodorus, the sixtieth illustration shows a rider on horseback, with his sword aloft and the horse elevating its front feet and the two young men, winged like angels, with scourges held aloft. These three agents of the godhead inflicted punishment on Heliodorus. The rider on horseback and the angel-like agents of divine retribution suggest resemblance to comparable figures in the Book of Revelation. Despite the emphasis in the illustration and commentary on sinful avarice, the implied virtuous counterpart to such depravity is charitable giving to the poor. In fact, the wealth in the temple of Jerusalem that Heliodorus sought to expropriate was donated, in part, by a wealthy man for the care of widows and orphans. God's approval of such charity and the divine intervention to protect the fund, not to mention Heliodorus's penitential experience after having suffered from divinely ordained affliction, all converge to emphasize the virtue of giving generously to others in need. As background to an understanding of Christ's flogging of the moneychangers, the episode involving Heliodorus brings light to the evil of the Pharisees, who situated the moneychangers, their agents, in the temple in order to lend funds to those persons seeking to buy sacrificial offerings. Receiving small gifts, on the one hand, and monetary interest from such loans, on the other, the moneychangers and the Pharisees whom they represented violate the account in Ezechiel 18.8 of the virtuous man, who does not lend money at interest nor exact usury. They also violate the injunction of Jesus in Luke 6.35, who urges that one lend money but expect nothing back. The larger theme of the commentary is the danger of riches and materialism and the prostitution of the temple of the Lord.

Chapter 16

Figure 61. Christ eats the Paschal lamb with his disciples

Affirming that Jesus instituted the Eucharist during the Last Supper, the emphasis here is on that Paschal meal as an "everlasting memorial." Recounted in Matthew 26.26–30, Mark 14.12–26, Luke 22.7–20, John 13.1–20, the Last Supper promotes sacramental and liturgical significance, for its reenactment in later eras both commemorates and celebrates the activity of Christ and his disciples. Evident in the illustration is the Paschal lamb at the center of the table, the meal that Jesus is blessing. The lamb signifies Christ's role as the *Agnus Dei*, or lamb of God. The knives suggest the metal, whether the nails at the Crucifixion or the Roman centurion's lance, which cut into the flesh of Jesus. The goblet from which a woman is drinking is presumably the cup that Jesus upheld and in which, as he announces, he offered his blood for the forgiveness of sins. The emphasis of the commentary is on the bread through which Jesus presents himself in the form of food, which is likened to, but contrasted with, the manna in the wilderness. Whereas the manna prefigures the Eucharist, the love of the Lord for his people, though great when they were in the wilderness, is greater because of the sacrament instituted at the Last Supper. Manna was granted at a time and in a particular place to alleviate hunger, but the Eucharist is "a bread that is eternal." If, in short, manna is an Old Testament prefiguration or type, then the Eucharist is the fulfillment or antitype in the New Dispensation. The commentary does not cite John 6, which includes the discourse by Jesus on the bread of life. But that discourse is the most sustained and detailed analysis of the typological interrelationship of manna in the desert and Jesus himself as "the bread of life," which he likens to his own flesh, a meal that results in eternal life.

Figure 62. Manna is given to the children of Israel in the desert

This illustration and commentary continue to explain the significance of manna as a context for understanding the greater significance of the Eucharist. The illustration shows the manna descending from clouds above, like bread from heaven. In Exodus 16.31, manna is likened to coriander seed but only with reference to size and shape (small and round) not taste and color. Both men and women gather the manna and place it in containers with the capacity of one omer, approximately a present-day gallon size receptacle. Accompanying the manna were drops of dew, which the commentary interprets as the grace that accompanies the Eucharist. Typological comparisons abound between manna and the Eucharist, but the commentary also focuses on the contrasts. Thus, the white manna signifies the purity of heart of the communicant. Whereas manna, as Wisdom 16.20 stipulates, delights the individual tastes of the people who eat it, the taste to which the Eucharist appeals is that of heavenly bliss, a prelude of which is achieved through meditation and contemplation, not to mention mysticism. Citing the Transfiguration and Peter's reaction to it (Matthew 17.1–4), the commentary indicates that a vision of heavenly bliss impels the disciple to offer to build three tabernacles — one for Jesus, another for Moses, and a third for Elias. Moses as the lawgiver and Elias as a prophet were on either side of Jesus during the Transfiguration on Mt. Tabor, thereby indicating, respectively, that the law of the Old Testament and the Hebraic prophecies concerning the advent of the Messiah were being fulfilled by the ministry of Jesus. This glimpse of Jesus — whose effulgence atop the mountain was a sign of his divinity — impelled Peter to designate the site as holy and to honor it by the construction of tabernacles. Jesus, on the other hand, was orienting his disciples heavenward, an orientation that occurs when one glimpses or partakes of divinity at the Eucharist.

Figure 63. The Jews eat the Paschal lamb

Drawn from Exodus 12.3–11, the illustration and commentary deal
with the ritual of Passover as stipulated by the Lord. Commanded
to slaughter a yearling, whether a goat or lamb, without blemish,
and to apply some of its blood to their doorposts and lintels, the
Israelites were protecting themselves and their families from the
death to be inflicted on the firstborn, whether man or beast. Though
the commentary does not cite these details, they nevertheless prefigure the Eucharist, which, as the flesh and blood of Christ, rescues humankind from the spiritual death of sinfulness. The image
of the bloodied doorpost and lintel is cross-like, suggesting that the
sacramental significance of the Last Supper — whereby Jesus offers
his flesh and blood — is validated at the Crucifixion. While they ate
the Paschal meal, which included the roasted animal, unleavened
bread, and bitter herbs, the Jews were to be prepared for flight out
of Egypt — their loins girt or cinctured, their feet shodden, staves
in hand, and standing erect. The illustration shows the readiness of
the Jews for flight as they prepare to partake of the Paschal meal.
In addition to the roasted animal, bitter herbs, resembling lettuce,
are on the table. The commentary correlates the details of the Exodus
event and the ritual of the Paschal meal with the readiness of communicants to partake of the Eucharist. What unfolds is a typological interpretation. Accordingly, the communicants are girded with
chastity; the staff they hold for support is faith; they are erect in
order to persevere in the life of holiness on which they are embark-
ing; the distasteful herbs of the Paschal meal signify the bitter
contrition of the communicants; their shodden feet are protected
from the pleasurable sensations that lead to sinfulness; the roasted
Paschal animal represents the fiery zeal of charity that overtakes
the communicants.

Figure 64. Melchisedech offers bread and wine to Abraham

The chief text underlying this illustration and commentary is Genesis 14, which recounts how Abraham undertook a military expedi-
tion against Chodorlahomor, king of Elam, and his confederates.

These adversaries had abducted Abraham's nephew, Lot, and seized his possessions, not to mention their pillaging of other cities. Abraham, having prevailed against his adversaries, returned with Lot, other captives, and all of what had been plundered. At his return, Abraham encountered Melchisedech, king of Salem, who brought bread and wine to the victor and acknowledged him as having been blessed by God. Melchisedech also praises God for having favored Abraham by delivering his enemies unto him. Two other biblical texts also come into play: Psalm 110 and Hebrews 4–5. While Psalm 110 extols the Messiah in his three roles — priest, king, conqueror — Melchisedech is cited as a prefiguration chiefly of the first and somewhat of the second role. Not a Levite and not descended from Aaron, to whom God entrusted the priesthood, Melchisedech owes his sacerdotal status directly to appointment and anointment from God. Likewise, the letter to the Hebrews 4–5 emphasizes God's announcement of the sonship of Jesus, a public proclamation of his role as high priest, who during his temporal ministry performs sacerdotal duties, praying to the Lord and suffering and offering sacrifice, most notably himself, on behalf of humankind. Identified as the deity on earth, Jesus in his priesthood extends salvation to all who obey him through their acceptance of his message. The sacramental implications of Melchisedech's bread and wine are clearly priestly; and the commentary stresses that the order of the priesthood supersedes in dignity all of the following: imperial rulers, patriarchs, prophets, and even angels. Only the priest has the God-given power to transform bread into the body of Jesus, many times over; whereas the Virgin Mary gave birth but once to Christ.

Chapter 17

Figure 65. Christ fells his enemies with one word

Matthew 26.26–56 and John 18.1–13 provide the context here. Pictured is the arrest of Jesus in Gethsemane, which shows the guards recoiling from him after he acknowledges that he is Jesus of

Nazareth. He does so by saying simply: "I am." This particular event and the language that Jesus uses occur only in John's account, and the language by which Jesus affirms his identity — "I am" — accords with the emphasis on his divine nature in the fourth Gospel. Iterated time and again by Jesus, this language indicates his integration in the godhead, for God in appearing to Moses in the burning bush had spoken of himself in that same way: "I am who am." By affirming his divinity and projecting his power, Jesus momentarily awes his captors, whom Judas has led to him. Knowing of his mission of self-sacrifice, Jesus willingly allows himself to be taken captive, so that his arrest, followed by his trial, will lead in turn to his Passion and Crucifixion. His death consummates the Eucharistic celebration that he had recently enacted with his disciples at their meal. The commentary contrasts the malice of Judas with the kindness and mercy of Jesus, particularly after that disciple had participated treacherously in the Last Supper. The commentary also stresses the relative impotence of armed captors, whose numbers and confidence in their weaponry were subdued by the humble and gentle presence of Jesus. Whether by treachery or through physical force, evil will yield to the greater power of goodness. This means that God foresees the role of evil in an overall Providential plan. What happens is that greater and greater manifestations of goodness eventuate from the opposition and seeming triumphs of evil, which are short-lived, for Doomsday will signal the final defeat of evil and the eternal triumph and celebration of goodness.

Figure 66. Samson fells a thousand with the jawbone of an ass

Judges 15.15–17 relates how Samson slew 1,000 Philistines with the jawbone of an ass. Samson accomplished his feat by the power that God infused in him. The feat, moreover, was one of several such actions that overcame vast numbers of Philistines. The emphasis in the scriptural account of Samson highlights the supremacy of divine intervention over any and all earthly power. The illustration depicts divine intervention at work through one of God's chosen ministers, Samson. The commentary presents numerous other examples of divine power, some more catastrophic than Samson's triumph over 1,000 enemies, notably the annihilation of Sodom and Gomorrha, the plagues visited on the Egyptians, and the destruction of Sennacherib's army of almost 200,000 warriors. These analogues stress, by contrast, the power of Jesus, who himself is God, power that could have been exercised, though it was voluntarily restrained, against a relatively small band of captors. Because Jesus at his arrest in Gethsemane manifests his divine power to awe his captors, an account unique to John's Gospel, the episode harmonizes with the emphasis on his divinity in the fourth Gospel, not to mention his total integration and identification with the godhead. Accordingly, in the citations of retributive divine power in the Old Testament, the implication is that Jesus (in his divine role as the Son) participated as well as the Father in such intervention. Not simply staying his hand but reflecting both humility and gentleness, Jesus projects obedience to the Providential plan of salvation and consents to his upcoming suffering and Crucifixion. In the face of increasing adversity, his traits of patience and fortitude exemplify norms of conduct for suffering humankind.

Figure 67. Samgar kills 600 men with a ploughshare

Judges 3.31, the biblical context for this illustration and commentary, is simply a single-verse account of Samgar slaying 600 Philistines with an oxgoad, a prod used to guide oxen. The illustration, however, shows Samgar with a two-handed sword, one that resembles a plowshare. The very brief account of Samgar occurs as part of a biblical catalog of the 12 judges (one of whom was Samson), whose military leadership of the Israelites at times resulted in remarkable victories against various enemies. These judges led one or more tribes of Israel, not the entire nation. They prefigure the coming of the monarchy and the kings of Israel. The saga of the Chosen People under the 12 judges contrasts the effects of obedience and disobedience of God. When the Israelites disobey God, they are victimized by oppressors. When they repent and obey God, he brings about their liberation by working through the judges, whom he invested with the power of victory. Only toward the end does the commentary on the illustration refer to Samgar, and then only briefly. Rather, the commentary dwells on other triumphs that God oversees through the kings of Israel and their prophets. And while these triumphs are military, God's power often afflicts the enemies of Israel to render their weapons useless or to maim or disable them physically. Such extensive and intensive emphasis on God's power serves as a backdrop to the gentleness of Christ, even to his captors, whom he momentarily awes. But obedient to his self-sacrificial ministry, Jesus willingly permits his enemies to regain control of themselves and to capture him. The larger theme, presumably, is the willingness of Jesus to accept death, after which his triumph over it is an even greater victory than all of the military successes of the Old Testament heroes raised up by God. The resurrection of Jesus, in short, and his intercession on behalf of humankind, who will triumph over death in his name, are the greatest victories.

Figure 68. David kills 800 men with his attack

The illustration shows David slaying 800 Philistines, and the biblical text cited is 2 Kings 23.8. Actually Scripture credits one of David's warriors, Ishbaal, with the slaying of the Philistines, a singlehanded exploit that he accomplished with what is described as a battle ax. While it continues the theme of heroic exploits that God inspires among the kings of the Chosen People and their warriors, the commentary uses David as an Old Testament prefiguration of another aspect of Christ's nature, gentleness. Balancing gentleness and severity in its comparative analysis of David and Christ, the commentary notes that David is mild in his domestic setting, but harsh with his enemies. Similarly, Christ reflects gentleness, patience, and fortitude, but in judging his enemies he is severe. Though the commentary does not specify the enemies as such, the implication is twofold: the immediate enemies of Jesus whom he identifies in his temporal ministry — namely, the Scribes and Pharisees; and the enemies, notably the reprobate, who reject

his offer of salvation, whom he will smite, so to speak, at Doomsday. The emphasis in the commentary, however, tends toward the
role of Jesus as willing sufferer, who accepts the harsh and cruel
punishment that they mete out to him. By unfolding in this manner, the commentary brings the gentleness of Jesus into greater
focus, for he suspends the justness of his severity against his enemies while tolerating their unjust severity against himself. The
irony in this interaction is that Jesus voluntarily subjects himself
to such humiliation on behalf of the very people who are inflicting
punishment on him. By rejecting his suffering for them, they in
effect are guilty of ingratitude and become self-willed reprobates.

Chapter 18

Figure 69. Christ is deceitfully betrayed

From Matthew 26.47–50, the illustration and commentary stress
the betrayal of Christ by Judas. Judas kisses Jesus, who is surrounded at once by armed captors. This is the crucial event in the
unfolding conspiracy of Judas with the priests and elders against
Jesus. The band of captors sent by the priests and elders took their
cue from Judas's kiss as the means of identifying Jesus. Describing
how Judas extends his right hand to touch or embrace Jesus while
kissing him, the commentary notes that the betrayer's left hand is
out of sight, surreptitiously drawing forth a dagger. While the reference to the dagger is figurative, the commentary makes clear that
under the guise of friendship, Judas pursues his treachery. The
embrace, the kiss, and the deferential speech all constitute the pretense under which Judas signals the captors to apprehend Jesus.
The commentary dwells on the ungrateful and insidious nature of
Judas, who had been chosen by Jesus to be part of his innermost
circle of 12 Apostles, with whom secrets were shared. By implication, "secrets" may refer to the special knowledge that Jesus imparted
to the Apostles — his prophecies, for example, concerning his death
and resurrection, the coming of the Paraclete, the Second Coming,

and the like. The Apostles, in other words, were inducted into the mysteries of the kingdom of God and entrusted to preach them, in turn, to all peoples. They were empowered to celebrate the Eucharist and in doing so to commemorate their fellowship with Jesus at the Last Supper. They witnessed the promise of Jesus to be with them — in effect, in their midst — for all days to come. The spiritual ministry that they were to enact, the converts whom they were to baptize, and the communities or churches that they were to found as evangelizers identify the Apostles as the veritable successors of Jesus. Despite this extraordinary status as a successor of Jesus, Judas still betrays him.

Figure 70. Joab kills his brother, Amasa

The seventieth illustration depicts an episode from 2 Kings 20.8–10, in which Joab treacherously slays Amasa, his brother. In the illustration, Joab extends his right hand in friendship to his brother, while furtively he removes his sword and stabs Amasa in the abdomen. The parallel with Judas's betrayal of Christ is clear. The commentary, however, focuses on the ingratitude of Judas, who rejects all of the powers, duties, authority, gifts, and trust that Jesus bestowed on him. One emphasis is on the presumed role of Judas as a bursar and steward of funds collected for almsgiving. But the commentary, in line with its characterization of Judas as a traitor and his well-known acceptance of the 30 pieces of silver, speculates on this aspect of his nature as an ongoing vice: venality. In other words, he betrayed the trust by filching funds that he was to have safeguarded. The pettiness of betraying Jesus for 30 pieces of silver accords with the view that Judas, earlier in the ministry of Jesus, also betrayed a larger trust for little materialistic compensation, tantamount to pilfering funds intended for almsgiving. The commentary continues to highlight the magnitude of Judas's betrayal. Having been granted the power to heal the sick and to cast out demons, Judas nevertheless turns over Christ to the captors. Having participated in the Last Supper and its Eucharistic celebration, Judas behaves treacherously toward Jesus. Though Jesus washed his feet, Judas betrays his master by kissing his cheek. While Jesus consents to the kiss of Judas, he does so despite his foreknowledge of the malice in the heart of his betrayer. Such a gesture of friendship by Jesus is a last effort to reclaim the betrayer, whose persistence in evil becomes finally self-damning.

Figure 71. King Saul gives David evil in return for goodness

Drawing on 1 Kings 19.9–10, this illustration shows David playing a cithara before the throne of Saul — an Old Testament analogue of the betrayal of Christ by Judas. The king, with the scepter in his left hand, has a drawn sword in his right, intending to slay David. Saul plots continually against David, who is warned by Jonathan, the king's son, of his father's sinister intent. The commentary cites the treachery and ingratitude of Saul toward David as prefigurations of the similar conduct of Judas toward Christ. Despite David's triumphs over the Philistines on behalf of Saul, the king persists in his malice toward his benefactor, even when he becomes his son-in-law. The plots against David continue. Similarly, Judas, despite the ongoing goodness of Jesus toward him, remains evil in return. Indeed, despite his foreknowledge of Judas's betrayal, Christ does not disclose his betrayer's identity to the other Apostles, who would have intervened against him. The commentary cites the Old Law's affirmation of retributive justice, so that the manifestation of evil by Judas in the face of goodness by Jesus could and should have resulted in justifiable revenge. The commentary also indicates that the Son assumed human nature, and Judas is accompanied by an armed band intent on apprehending Jesus and later on slaying him. By implication, such a statement recalls previous illustrations and commentaries in the blockbook whereby the Son manifests humility in his Incarnation, undertaken in order to offer himself sacrificially on behalf of fallen humankind. While the role of Judas is instrumental in leading to the death of Jesus, the commentary faults the traitor for choices that led to his own downfall; it does not present him as having been fated to do so.

Figure 72. Cain deceitfully kills his brother, Abel

Genesis 4.1–11 recalls the offerings of Cain and Abel to God, the Lord's rejection of the former and acceptance of the latter, and the consequent slaying of the younger brother by the older. The illustration of this scriptural account is twofold: first, to the viewer's left, Cain and Abel, respectively, have placed a firstborn animal from the flock and a sheaf of grain atop an altar of sacrifice; second, to the viewer's right, Cain attacks his unarmed brother. The commentary presents the slaying of Abel as the analogue of Saul's murderous impulses toward David. It likewise prefigures the treachery of Judas toward Jesus. In all three instances — the two from the Old Testament, the one from the New Testament — the victims of the treachery were innocent or, in the cases of David and Jesus, did remarkable acts of goodness toward those who betray them. In these particular cases, the malefactors are most insidious. The commentary cites John 11.48, wherein the chief priests and Pharisees at a meeting of the Sanhedrin acknowledged that many Jews put faith in Jesus, who if left alone would gain other believers. Their plot against him began at that point, for if left unchecked, Jesus, they feared, would destroy the Jewish religion and nation. The commentary emphasizes the truth of Christ's preaching and dwells on the fact that the Son, being one with the Father, was the creator of humankind and later when he assumed the human nature and form became Jesus Christ. As such, he is both the father and brother of humankind. So his death, in which Judas played a part, constitutes both patricide and fratricide. Despite the cruelty shown toward him, the commentary invokes Jesus to be merciful.

Chapter 19

Figure 73. Christ is blindfolded, spit upon, and beaten

Whereas Mark 15.16–20 and Matthew 27.27–31 provide the longest descriptions of the buffeting of Jesus, Luke 22.63–65 and John

19.2–3 comment also on this humiliation of Christ. In fact, Luke's Gospel is the only one to mention the blindfolding of Jesus. In the present illustration, three tormentors pummel and expectorate on Jesus, while deriding him as the so-called king of the Jews. Seated and invested with a garment intended to be royal in appearance, Jesus, without a blindfold, crosses his hands on his lap, a prefiguration of his imminent death by crucifixion, the consummate cruelty of his Passion. One of the tormentors kneels before Jesus, pretending to pay homage, as if he were presenting a petition to a king enthroned in a chair of state. Absent from the illustration are the crown of thorns and the reed that Jesus was given to serve as his scepter. The commentary situates this particular episode in the greater context of the Passion, including reference to the arrest of Jesus and his trial at the Sanhedrin before the chief priests, scribes, and elders. The commentary notes that even at his arrest Jesus is gentle. When Peter tries to protect him from being captured and cuts off the ear of one of his captors, whom John 18.10 identifies as Malchus, Jesus performs a miracle of healing on the victim. This act, recorded only in Luke 22.50–51, highlights by contrast the cruelty of the enemies of Jesus. Proceeding next to the interrogation and trial of Jesus, the commentary notes that when replying to one of the high priest's questions (John 18.22), Jesus was struck in the face by a guard, who was believed to be the very one whose ear was restored. In suggesting that Malchus and the guard who strikes Jesus during the interrogation by Annas are the same person, the commentary focuses on the cruelty, ingratitude, and evil of the enemies of Christ.

Figure 74. Miriam's husband Hur is suffocated by the spittle of the Jews

Chiefly relying on Peter Comestor's *Historia Scholastica* (*PL*, CXCVIII, 1189–1190), the seventy-fourth illustration shows Hur overwhelmed by the spittle of his fellow Jews. Hur, whose wife was Miriam, the sister of Moses, challenged the Israelites' worship of the golden calf; in reprisal, they humiliated him. Without specific reference to Hur's experience, the commentary focuses on the insults, injuries, and abuses that Jesus undergoes in the events leading to the Crucifixion. In the buffeting to which the commentary refers, the blindfolded Jesus is asked who is striking him. His tormentors are playing a harsh version of a game called buffeting the blind(folded) man, or blind man's buff (also called blind man's bluff). The blindfolded victim must identify or catch (in a variation of tag) one of his tormentors, who cannot be seen or who disguises his voice. Extolled are the patience of Jesus, a virtue enabling him to withstand increasing adversity, and his mercy, which he extends toward his merciless captors and tormentors. Though blindfolded, Jesus as the godhead is omniscient, and he not only knows his tormentors but also forgives them. At its conclusion, the commentary identifies the hands of Jesus bound by his tormentors as the very hands that executed the primal act of the Creation, which resulted, among other things, in the heavens and the earth. By implication, the commentary presents the Son as the agent of the triune godhead at the Creation. To undergo the torment inflicted by his captors, the Son suppresses that very omnipotence that he exercised in the act of the Creation. By placing himself, in effect, under the power of the creatures that owe their existence to him, the Son manifests humility and uniquely profound love and mercy toward them.

Figure 75. Ham mocks his father, Noe, whereas the other brothers pity him

Genesis 9.1, 18–23 provides the context for an illustration that shows Ham mocking his inebriated father, Noe. Before dealing with the episode of the illustration, the commentary cites certain ironies associated with the buffeting of Jesus. First, that the Lord, who inspired the prophets, is tormented and urged to play the prophet, as Luke 22.64 records, by identifying his attackers though he is blindfolded. Second, that the Lord who led the Israelites during the Exodus, preceding them by means of a cloud in the daytime and a pillar of light at night, should have his eyes covered by a cloth and his face with spittle. Third, that Hur in opposing the Jewish idola-

ters undergoes a fate that anticipates some of the humiliation Jesus
suffers when he falls victim to the anger of the Pharisees, whose
teachings he challenged. Turning then to the illustration, the commentary perceives the dishonoring of Noe as a prefiguration of the
abuse directed at Jesus. A correspondence, though not cited by
the commentary, includes the exposure of Noe to his son, Ham, and
the ridicule of Jesus, who is partially nude when scourged, an event
that Mark 15.15, Matthew 27.26, and John 19.1 record as having
occurred immediately before the buffeting. Another correspondence
involves the unconsciousness of Noe and the fatigue and faintness
of Jesus from pain and the loss of blood at the scourging and buffeting. Not to be overlooked in the illustration is the vineyard in the
background, with its clusters of grapes, which a goat is eager to eat.
Because Genesis 9.20 describes Noe as a tiller of the soil and the
planter of the first vineyard, this sign of fertility in Nature mirrors
the generational propagation that God forecasts for Noe in Genesis
9.1–7. The descendants of Noe, in other words, will fill the earth, so
much so that they constitute the biblical catalogs of Genesis 10.
These peoples will, after the manner of a fertile grapevine, branch
out and spread over the earth.

Figure 76. After having blinded Samson, the Philistines make a fool of him

Judges 16.20–30 supplies the basis for the illustration and commentary, which together present the climax of Samson's career as a
Judge. Samson, having been captured, blinded, and ridiculed by the
Philistines, anticipates the arrest of Jesus, the darkening of his
vision by the blindfold during the buffeting, and the derision. If
Samson is comparable to Jesus in the humiliation he suffers, he also
anticipates Jesus's vengeance against his enemies, the reprobates.
The illustration shows Samson at the mainstay of support, where-
on the temple of Dagon, the god of the Philistines, rested. When
Samson, whose strength returned with the regrowth of his hair,
pushed against the mainstay, it collapsed, and the temple disintegrated.
In this consummate act, Samson while killing himself also slays

more Philistines than he had by his previous exploits. The commentary presents this consummate act as the fullest revenge of Samson, who had previously permitted himself to be bound, a reference presumably to Judges 15.12–15, when his own people tied his arms with ropes and delivered him to the Philistines. Breaking the bonds, however, Samson took up the jawbone of an ass to slay multitudes of his enemies. The commentary views Samson's various punishments against the Philistines as prefigurations of the vengeance that Jesus will mete out to the reprobate at Doomsday, who will prefer to be sped directly to their torment, rather than even confront the angry visage of the all-knowing judge. The commentary ends on a positive note that heralds the sanctified souls and their eternal bliss, urging humankind to heed the summons of the Lord to salvation.

Chapter 20

Figure 77. Jesus is tied to a column and scourged

Here the blockbook draws on Mark 15.15, Matthew 27.26, John 19.1–2 but also so on Peter Comestor's *Historia Scholastica* (*PL*, CXCVIII, 1628), dealing with the scourging of Christ. The nudity of Jesus, his eventual exhaustion from severe pain and loss of blood, and the cross-like configuration of his bound hands all anticipate the more extreme torment of the crucifixion. The commentary focuses on the interrogation and trial of Jesus, conducted variously by Pilate and Herod but also recalling the roles of Annas and Caiphas as questioners and judges. Their roles are crucial in understanding the hostile tone of the people toward Jesus, the climate in which Pilate renders his judgments. John 11.45–54 explains how Caiphas at the Sanhedrin urged that Jesus be put to death, a loss of one man rather than the destruction of the Jewish nation, which would have resulted as Jesus elicited the attention and faith of more and more Jews. Mark 14.53–65, Matthew 26.57–68, Luke 22.63–71, and John 18.19–24 recount the roles of the Jewish priests in inciting the crowd against Jesus, a situation that frightens even Pilate (John 19.8) and causes him to give Jesus over to the rabble, rather than free him. Luke 23.6–12 records that Herod also speaks with Jesus, anticipating the enactment of a miracle. Jesus, however, remained silent under the questioning, which was conducted while the Jewish priests directed vehement accusations at him. The commentary also interprets the Holy Spirit's twofold presence in the conspiracies leading to Jesus' death. Before Jesus is dismissed, Herod has him dressed in a white garment, a sign of innocence. Similarly, when Caiphas before the Sanhedrin had proposed the loss of one man, namely Jesus, in order to save the nation, so to speak, his comments resonate with irony beyond his comprehension, most notably concerning the sacrificial and salvific ministry of Christ.

Figure 78. Holofernes's servant ties Prince Achior to a tree

From the Book of Judith 5.5–29, 6.7–13, this illustration shows Achior, leader of the Ammonites, who appraises the Israelites. Holofernes, commander of the Assyrians, sought military intelligence concerning the Israelites, whom he was about to attack. Essentially, Achior reports that the deity of the Israelites will protect his people if they are faithful to him; when they are unfaithful, however, they are vulnerable to their enemies, who will prevail over them. They will become abased as captives in foreign lands. Confident that he will triumph over the Israelites and encouraged by Achior's appraisal of the Israelites as an affront to his military supremacy, Holofernes orders the spy turned over to the Israelites, in whom he had so much confidence, so that he will be slain along with them. Bound at the base of a mountain, Achior is liberated by the Israelites who welcome him.

The commentary shows that Pilate, having considered the allegations against Christ, finds the captive to be innocent. Despite his findings, Pilate, intimidated by the crowd and eager to appease them, has Jesus scourged. As their demands for the life of Jesus become more vehement, Pilate turns him over to the Jews for crucifixion.

Jesus' helplessness, like that of Achior, distinguishes him as a victim. What is also crucial in the interrogation and trial of Jesus is the finding that he is innocent of political subversion, a major feature promulgated by Pilate. Advocating neither disobedience toward Rome, nor claiming to be King of Judea, and all the while contending that his so-called kingdom is not of the present world, Jesus continues to defy the misperceptions of Romans and Jews alike concerning his ministry on earth. Posing no threat whatsoever to the extant political order and to the imperial hegemony of Rome, Jesus should not have been perceived as a serious antagonist.

Figure 79. Lamech is held in check by his evil wives

Genesis 4.18–19 and Peter Comestor's *Historia Scholastica* (*PL*, CXCVIII, 1079) furnish the background here. Pictured is Lamech, whose two wives assail him verbally and physically. The commentary likens their abuse to the dual antagonism of (1) pagans who pummel Jesus with instruments of torture and (2) the populace of the synagogue who verbally thrash him. Against the context of Achior's isolation and punishment, as well as Lamech's humiliation, the two flagellations of Jesus — one physical, the other verbal — come into focus. Significantly, the commentary also cites Job 2, wherein the physical punishment that Satan wreaks on Job — the festering boils across his person — tests his self-affirmed belief in his innocence and his concomitant faith in the Lord. Added thereto is his wife's questioning of her husband's innocence. If indeed he is innocent of wrongdoing, or sinless, then he should renounce and curse the Lord for the unjust suffering visited upon him. Maintaining his innocence of wrongdoing, withstanding increasing adversity, and curbing any temptation to inveigh against the Lord, Job serves as an Old Testament prefiguration of Christ at the Passion. Such comprehensive contexts, all of them Hebraic, shed light on the multilevel suffering that Jesus underwent, ranging from the physical, on the one hand, to the psychological, on the other. In withstanding such suffering, Jesus, like Job, exercises numerous virtues, notably faith in God and in one's unfolding role in Providential and redemptive history, patience, and fortitude. While these virtues are traditionally perceived as contemplative or passive, in a very real sense they become the features of Christian heroism, which is embodied in an exemplary manner by Jesus, though prefigured by Job.

Figure 80. Job is scourged by the devil and by his wife

Figure 80 shows Job being doubly scourged: by his own wife and by the devil. Whereas the devil wields an actual scourge, Job's wife uses a verbal whiplash. The devil imparts comprehensive pain, the scourge being a sign of the suffering from the boils that overtake him from the soles of his feet to the top of his head. Less active in her infliction of pain but, paradoxically, more devastating in her punishment, Job's wife tests his perception of himself as innocent while she calls attention to how unfortunate he has become. Noting the disparity between his contention of innocence and the depth of his misfortune, she questions Job's steadfast faith in the Lord. Such a challenge would tend to erode one's faith, cause one to accuse the Lord of injustices, tempt one to become a blasphemer, and urge one to assail the Lord as perversely disloyal to his servants. However much one is challenged along these lines, the commentary stresses that he or she should turn to Jesus himself as the exemplar of faith, patience, and fortitude, whose innocence makes his punishment all the more severe and who undergoes affliction on behalf of fallen humankind. In the framework of Jesus' sacrifice, the so-called good works of humankind are questioned as to their value and validity, particularly with reference to justification and salvation. Relatively inconsequential, these good works pale by contrast with the sacrifice of Christ, from whom one drop of blood supersedes any man's cumulative total of good works. Rounding off the commentary is the plea for some suffering in the present life, which, as it informs the state of one's mind, heart, and soul, will assist in purging humankind of sinfulness and its consequences and expedite the transit of the soul from the present world directly to eternal bliss, without an intermediate station in Purgatory.

Chapter 21

Figure 81. Christ is crowned with thorns

The crowning with thorns is the central event, an episode recounted in all four Gospels (Matthew 27.27–30, Mark 15.16–20, Luke 23.11, John 19.1–3). This illustration depicts two tormentors of Jesus who use poles to press a crown of thorns onto his head as part of a mocking scenario that characterizes him as King of the Jews. Gazing downward to another tormentor, who while kneeling offers him derisively a reed as if it were a scepter, Jesus crosses his hands at the wrists, a foreshadowing of his death by crucifixion. His long and flowing robe, clasped at his neck, signifies royal attire, and his bench is akin to a throne or chair of state. The commentary dwells on the extraordinary punishment meted out to Jesus: an increased number of lashes at a scourging, a crowning with thorns, and multiple scourgings. Underlying this physical punishment, to be sure, is the psychological anguish of mockery and derision. Citing Luke 6.38 and its wordplay on "measure," which echoes in effect Mark 4.24, the commentary focuses on the apt and ironic retribution that will befall Christ's tormentors. What they have meted or measured out to Jesus as punishment, they will experience in return, not simply in even proportion but exponentially greater. The implication is that the agonies of eternal damnation will be the measure of retribution against the reprobate. The corollary is that Jesus himself, who was on trial, will be the judge of his tormentors. At Doomsday and the Final Judgment, he will be enthroned on high, judging humankind as saved or damned. In doing so, he will be measuring their lives against the so-called doctrine of the cross that he preached and lived during his temporal ministry — whether humankind accepted or rejected his call to suffering and humiliation as the means to eternal triumph and exaltation.

Figure 82. The concubine takes the king's crown and crowns herself

Derived chiefly from the Apocrypha, 1 Esdras 4.29 (see *The Apocrypha and Pseudepigraphia of the Old Testament*, ed. R. H. Charles [Oxford, 1913], vol. 1, 31), the illustration portrays a concubine of King Darius, who removes his crown and places it on her own head. This act, which at first glance appears to be the arrogation of kingship by another, has greater significance in its denial of the glory and sovereignty that are due to a legitimate ruler. Even more than that, however, the commentary focuses on the ingratitude of humankind, which is all the more egregious because it repays the kindness of the sovereign Lord with insult, injury, and even death. The commentary cites events associated with the crowning with thorns but interprets them as individual and sequential acts of cruelty ironically counteracting the loving acts of the Lord as benevolent sovereign to his Chosen People. Examples abound, including the Lord's scourging of the Pharao and the Egyptians, but humankind's scourging of the Lord; and the Lord's breaking of the crown or hegemony of the king of Egypt over the Chosen People, but humankind's bestowal of a crown of thorns on the Lord; and the Lord's empowerment of small numbers of his Chosen People who dispel thousands of adversaries, but humankind's depravity whereby two realms — Rome and Judea — conspire against him. More fundamentally, the commentary while citing the tormentor of Jesus who genuflects while offering a reed, perceives this ritualistic gesture as a mockery of the traditional attitude by which one pays homage or presents a gift to a king. From this perspective, the visitation of the Magi to Jesus, their genuflection in homage to him, and their presentation of gifts constitute a frame of reference against which the mockery of Jesus at the crowning with thorns comes into focus.

Figure 83. Semei curses David

From 2 Kings 16.5–14, the illustration depicts Semei cursing and throwing stones and dirt at David and calling the king a murderer because of the bloodshed that he wrought in the house of Saul, in whose stead he became king. Though David's followers urged the king to silence Semei, even to the point of slaying him, David was more patient and prudent. Recognizing the possibility that the Lord incited Semei to curse David for wrongdoing, the king tolerates, even encourages, the invective directed at himself. Using both Darius's concubine and Semei as analogues for the tormentors who abuse Christ during the crowning with thorns, the commentary extols the patience and meekness of Christ. These traits are prefigured by King Darius's ongoing love of his concubine, despite her abuse of him, and by King David's tolerance of invective and physical assault. In a larger sense, the commentary celebrates the patience and fortitude associated with humiliation, rather than the active resistance to punishment and exercise of heroic strength that would enable one to overthrow his adversaries. The aim is to dramatize the depth of Christ's love for his tormentors. His voluntary humiliation not only suppresses his divine omnipotence but also renders him vulnerable to suffering at the very hands of the people whom he continues to love. As they torment him, such ingratitude elicits further manifestation of his love, a curious, indeed unique, phenomenon. In this transaction, the greater the torment that Christ undergoes, the more profound an expression of love he pays forth. He does so not simply in the historical context of his crucifixion but also throughout the panorama of time, continuing to love tormentors or sinners whom he foreknows will finally reject his redemptive act on their behalf.

Figure 84. King Hanon dishonors David's messengers

The episodes in 2 Kings 10.2–5 furnish the framework for figure 84. In the illustration one of King David's couriers undergoes abuse — the shaving of his beard and the cutting away of his garment. David sent the couriers to express condolences to King Hanon, whose father had recently died. But the king, having been swayed by his counselors, imputed sinister motives to David's couriers, perceiving them as spies. He, therefore, mistreated them, a situation that resulted in warfare. In using this context to interpret the crowning with thorns, the commentary stresses the mediation of Christ to reestablish peace between the godhead and humankind. Such mediation takes the form of self-sacrifice by Christ, a peacemaker who is derided, ironically, by the very persons on whose behalf he offers himself. The commentary cites, however briefly, both pagan and Jewish forms of sacrifice and libation, variously involving blood and water or their combination. But the issuance of water and blood from Christ's side at the crucifixion is the consummate gesture of both sacrifice and libation. That is, the emissions from his sacrificed body become the very libations for anointing, or for regenerating fallen humankind. The water and blood from Christ's side bear on the so-called mystical origins of the sacraments of Baptism and the Eucharist. Whereas the sacrament of initiation by cleansing and restoring humankind to pristine holiness is more purgative in its effect, the Eucharist when imbibed as a drink imparts grace. The intake of grace by this means suggests an infusion of divine assistance, which the godhead may choose to grant as a gift to humankind in a state of spiritual readiness.

Chapter 22

Figure 85. Christ carries his cross

Matthew 27.31, Mark 15.20, and John 19.16–17 center upon the frenzy of the populace to crucify Jesus, Pilate's capitulation to their wishes, and the carrying of the cross by Jesus as part of his *via dolorosa*, or sorrowful way, to Golgotha. In this corresponding illustration, Jesus carries the cross under the watchful eyes of two attendants. The one behind Jesus places the upright beam on his right shoulder and against the right side of his neck, with the transverse beam resting and pressing downward on the back or nape of his neck. It appears that the head of Jesus is wedged in the intersection of the upright and transverse beams of the cross, a sign of his inexorable destiny, with which he obediently complies. The attendant in front holds a rope that is fastened to the waist of Jesus in order to lead him along his journey to Calvary. In his other hand, the attendant holds a hammer with which to nail Jesus to the cross. In the background are two peaks, one of which may be Calvary.

The commentary emphasizes how Pilate proclaims the innocence of Jesus and even reminds the populace that at Passover he customarily releases a prisoner. Rather than Jesus, the crowd prefers the release of the insurrectionist, Barabbas. Because of the frenzy of the crowd, Pilate hands over Jesus to them for crucifixion. The commentary also focuses on the interplay of the Holy Spirit and the devil in Pilate's process of deciding the fate of Jesus. When Pilate seeks to persuade the Jews not to advocate the death of Jesus, the commentary presents him as having been instigated by the devil, who strives to thwart the plan of salvation. That plan, to be sure, depends on the sacrificial death of Jesus. When, on the other hand, Pilate delivers Jesus, whom he declared innocent and just, to the Jews for crucifixion, the commentary interprets this action as having fallen under the influence of the Holy Spirit. In this way, the redemptive ministry of Jesus will be consummated.

Figure 86. Isaac carries the wood for his sacrifice

This illustration and commentary center upon the intended sacrifice of Isaac by Abraham as recounted in Genesis 22.6–15. Depicted are Abraham, with sword drawn, and Isaac, who is kneeling on an Old Testament altar of sacrifice, head bowed forward. An angel by intervening prevents the sacrifice of Isaac, so that the holocaust to have taken place is forestalled. The wood for burning the offering rests on the ground alongside the altar. Some of the twigs are crossed, thereby prefiguring the crucifix as the site of Christ's sacrifice. Abraham's sword prefigures the metal — whether the nails or the lance of the centurion — that entered Christ. The travel of Isaac — who, according to Scripture, bore on his shoulders the wood for the holocaust — anticipates Christ's carrying of the cross, and the site of the altar atop Mount Moriah prefigures Calvary.

The commentary deals with the transformation in humankind's

perception of the cross, which was a means of punishing brigands. But when used for the execution of Jesus, the cross was ennobled, so to speak. It became, as well, a sign of the new faith, Christianity, the very sign traced on the foreheads of the faithful. The cross as a site of triumph by Jesus over Satan makes it a glorified instrument. Jesus, by consummating his redemptive ministry on the cross, nullifies the power of Satan over the souls of the Old Dispensation who are in limbo. Iconographically, the cross of suffering and humiliation gives way to a cross of triumph to reflect the transition from *Christus Patiens* (or the suffering Christ) to *Christus Victor* (or the victorious Christ). When at the harrowing of hell Jesus releases from captivity the souls of the Old Dispensation, he often appears with a lance-like cross, atop which a pennon is affixed, often with an emblazoned red cross. Whereas the cross of suffering and humiliation inflicted punishment on him, his triumphal cross is one of the *arma Christi* (or weapons of Christ) deployed against Satan.

Figure 87. The heir of the vineyard is cast out and killed

The parable of the tenants (Matthew 21.33–44) informs this illustration and commentary. In the illustration are a fertile vineyard, a wall, and a tower, though Scripture recounts that a winepress was also nearby. Inside the vineyard are tenants to whom the lord entrusted his vineyard. But at the harvest when he sends his servants to claim his share of the grapes, the tenants brutally slay them and others whom the lord sends. Finally, he sends his son, whom the tenants treat more savagely; for, Scripture states, they perceive him as the lord's heir. By killing him, they hope to usurp his inheritance. The commentary states that Jesus by such a parable forecasts humankind's rejection and savage treatment of him. The commentary, moreover, situates the parable in a broader context, one deriving in part from the story of Abraham and Isaac, in whose stead a ram, its horns caught in a thicket, is sacrificed. Whereas the ram as a holocaust is substituted for Isaac, Christ alone is sacrificed for all of humankind's sins. This willingness to be sacrificed emerges as well in deliberations among the Persons of the triune godhead. The commentary frames these deliberations as a consult of sorts involving the Father, Son, and Holy Spirit, from whose ranks one will be sent to redeem humankind. The Son volunteers to be the redeemer, in response to the Father's query, which is posed among and to the Divine Persons. The Father in acknowledging the role of the Son as redeemer instructs him to dwell among men and to bear patiently whatever they do to him. As such, the Son Incarnate will become *Christus Patiens* or the suffering but patient Christ.

Figure 88. The spies carry a cluster of grapes on a pole

Numbers 13.23–28 furnishes the basis here. Moses dispatched 12 scouts, one from each ancestral tribe, to reconnoiter the land of Canaan, especially to learn more about the people already inhabiting it and about the nature of the soil, whether barren or fruitful, wooded or clear. In the illustration two scouts, having cut a cluster of grapes as evidence of the fertility of Canaan, transport their bounty to Moses. The grapes are suspended from a pole that rests on the shoulders of the two scouts, each of whom has a walking stick. In the commentary, the two scouts represent the Jews and the Gentiles, who together carry the stalk of grapes, which signify Jesus, from Jerusalem to Calvary.

In this interpretive framework, the grapes, which are rich with juice, become the sacramental drink. The inveterate image of the winepress of the cross comes into play by implication. The bounty of the stalk of grapes and of the juice issuing from them speaks to the unlimited supply of Christ's bloodshed, whose efficacy as saving grace extends to sinners of the past, present, and future. Among the ironies in depicting saving grace as a stalk of grapes is the necessity to press the fruit in order to produce the juice. By being sinful, humankind in effect turns the screw on the winepress of the cross in order to crush the stalk of grapes. The more sinful humankind is, the greater the production of juice. In other words, Christ is more loving when he yields more blood. For such to occur, the punishment inflicted on him must be more prolonged and more torturous, a condition that results from humankind's ongoing and heinous sinfulness.

Chapter 23

Figure 89. The crucified Christ predicts his death

From Matthew 27.32–37, Mark 15.21–26, Luke 23.26–34, and John 19.17–18, this deals with the last episodes in the crucifixion of Jesus, including the enlistment of Simon of Cyrene to assist with the carrying of the cross. The illustration depicts Jesus, recumbent and divested of his outer garments, being nailed to the cross, after which it will be elevated. The commentary cites the Psalms as anticipations of the crucifixion, particularly the prefigurative language in these Old Testament songs: first, concerning the drink of gall provided Jesus who indicates that he is thirsty (Psalms 68.22); and, second, the stretching that he undergoes before his left and right hands, as well as his feet, are nailed to the cross. Because of this tension in his body, his bones become visible, lending credence to the Psalmic prophecy that his tormentors will number the bones of the Lord (Psalms 21.17–18). Despite the torment, Jesus, among his last utterances, prays that his torturers may be forgiven (Luke 23.24). As such, he exemplifies both mercy and charity, and serves thereby as a model for loving one's enemies. Though the commentary does not develop the point, the stretched sinews and bones of Jesus on the cross, particularly in the broader context of the Psalms, may be likened to a musical instrument. Like the lyre of David, to whom many of the Psalms are attributed, the taut body of Jesus on the cross generates sighs and groans or the sounds of suffering but also hymns of mercy and charity on behalf of his tormentors. This gamut of music informs the tonal range of hymnology on Good Friday, which will give way, in turn, to the jubilation associated with the Resurrection.

Figure 90. The inventors of the arts of working with metals and making melodies

Genesis 4.21–22 identifies Jubal as the ancestor of all who play the lyre and pipe, and Tubalcain as the ancestor of all who forge instruments of bronze and iron. Accordingly, the ninetieth illustration and

commentary center on these two arts — music and metal work —
and their use in the crucifixion. In the illustration Tubalcain oversees blacksmiths who, having removed with tongs a piece of metal
from the forge, rest it on an anvil, then pound it with their hammers
into the shape and for the use that they desire. The commentary
states that Jubal, who overhears the workers' hammers striking the
iron, invented music from those sounds. By implication, the commentary indicates that the sounds of metal striking metal are
echoed by the executioners' hammers that drive the nails into Christ
on the cross. To this so-called instrumental music, Jesus provides
lyrical accompaniment when he prays that the Father may forgive
the executioners, a chant of mercy and love that becomes a pleasant song of intercession on behalf of the malefactors.

While the commentary links that intercessory song by Jesus to
the conversion of 3,000 at that very hour, there is no scriptural evidence of such an effect. More likely, the reference is to Acts 2.41,
which describes Peter's preaching on the topics of the crucified and
risen Lord. That message, which echoes the forgiveness of Christ's
intercessory song, is favorably received by a crowd of 3,000, whose
baptism by Peter is a sign of their conversion. The invention of
music and the crucifixion having been interrelated, the commentary then proceeds to associate the work of the first ironmakers and
the innovative means of Christ's crucifixion. Prior to the execution
of Christ, ropes, rather than nails, were used to suspend a victim,
until death, from the cross. The irony is that the ingenuity or in-
ventive capability of humankind is put to perverse use: to devise a
more torturous means of death for the Lord.

Figure 91. Isaias the prophet is cut in half by a saw

A legendary account of the martyrdom of Isaias, who is cut in two,
appears in the Apocrypha (see *The Apocrypha and Pseudepigraphia
of the Old Testament*, ed. R. H. Charles [Oxford, 1913], II, 159–62)
and in Peter Comestor's *Historia Scholastica* (*PL*, CXCVIII, 1414).
As a prophet associated with the messianic oracles, which foresaw
the passion and glorification of Christ, Isaias according to legendary

accounts and by sympathetic anticipation suffered a torturous death that prefigured what would befall Christ many centuries later. Like Christ, moreover, Isaias preached of sinfulness, expiation, and the restoration of faith in the Lord. The illustration of the prophet's execution shows Isaias upside down, his feet attached by a rope to a pole. Two executioners, on either side of Isaias, position a handsaw with large serrated teeth between his legs and begin to cut through his lower abdomen. From one vantage point, the attitude of Isaias at his execution resembles the stalk of grapes suspended from the pole that the scouts bear when they return from Canaan, and the bloodshed Isaias will shed in martyrdom is akin to the juice from the crushed grapes. To be sure, the stalk of grapes and Isaias, as object and personage respectively, prefigure Christ crucified and the bloodshed of the Redemption. The commentary also dwells on the sawing of Isaias in two as the basis for understanding the indivisible union of two natures in Christ, the human and divine. When Christ dies, his body is separated from his soul, a disunion that occurs in all humankind at death. But the commentary stresses that even the death of Christ does not bring about a separation of his divinity either from his body or from his soul. The hypostatic union of divinity and humanity remains intact in Christ and his two natures continue to be inseparable.

Figure 92. King Moab sacrifices his son on the wall

Chiefly from 4 Kings 3.26–27, this illustration and commentary feature Mesha, the king of Moab, sacrificing his firstborn son. Suffering great losses in his battle against the Israelites, who also razed many towns in his kingdom and conducted a systematic despoliation of the land, the king of Moab, undergoing siege in the capital of his kingdom and anticipating defeat by the Israelites, escorted his eldest son to the walls of the city and sacrificed him in full view. Scripture indicates that indignation and wrath against the Israelites were so great that they broke off the siege and returned home. This scriptural account raises several possible interpretations. One interpretation centers on the wrath of the Moabite god, to whom the son was sacrificed, wrath directed against the Israelites who then lost their courage on foreign land and sought thereafter to return to their homeland. Another interpretation deals with the wrath aroused in the Moabites as a reaction to the sacrifice of their crown prince, an action that incited them to launch a counterattack that drove away the Israelites. From this perspective, one might surmise that the Moabite god used the fierce warriors who worshiped him as his instruments of wrath against the foreign invaders, the Israelites. The commentary distinguishes between the sacrifice of the king of Moab's son, which was undertaken for the friends and subjects of the Moabite kingdom, and God the Father's sacrifice of his Son for his enemies. In the light of previous illustrations and commentaries, the unique significance of God the Father's sacrifice of his Son stems from the forgiveness that Christ requests for his very tormentors. While undergoing punishment at their hands, Christ becomes a sacrificial offering on their behalf. Thus, Christ virtually endears himself to his enemies, whereas the Israelites are put to flight, presumably because of the wrath aroused against them by the sacrifice of the firstborn son of the king of the Moabites.

Chapter 24

Figure 93. Christ hangs from the cross

Luke 23.32–34 and John 19.18 are the only Gospels that mention that two criminals were crucified along with Jesus. This illustration and commentary present the cross as a tree, an analogy likewise reinforced by reference to Daniel 4, in which the entire chapter elaborates on the significance of Nebuchodonosor's dream of an enormous tree whose branches overspread the earth and whose summit reached heavenward. Interpreting Nebuchodonosor's dream as a mystical prefiguration of Christ's kingship, the commentary dwells on the power of the Lord that encompasses the world at large but also transcends it, for Christ the King has his realm in the hereafter. Despite the illustration that shows Christ crucified, seemingly the nadir of his humiliation, the crucifix and Christ outstretched on it encompass the two thieves — the one regenerate, the other unregenerate. Symbolic of all humankind — some to be saved, others to be damned — the two thieves prefigure Doomsday and the Final Judgment. Christ in session at his Second Coming, enthroned in power and glory, will judge humankind to be saved or damned according to their acceptance or rejection of the doctrine of the cross. Taking up the cross in the manner of Jesus and suffering humiliation in his name are the crucial elements in the doctrine of the cross. In fact, the two thieves in their dialogue with Jesus typify humankind's reaction to the message and ministry of Jesus. The unregenerate thief rebukes and derides Jesus, after the manner of the tormentors during the Passion, whereas the regenerate thief requests that Jesus, after having entered into his reign in the hereafter, remember him, an affirmation of the power of Christ the king.

Figure 94. In a dream Nebuchodonosor sees a tree

The story of Nebuchodonosor's dream comes from Daniel 4. The king is asleep, and his dream-vision is being enacted alongside his bed. In the branches of the tree, five birds appear, and the one at the summit (whose wings are outstretched) assumes an attitude typical of the Holy Spirit when zoomorphically rendered, or of a pelican that pricks its breast and nourishes its fledglings from the issuance of its own blood. Under the tree are animals standing in the shade or grazing on the grass. Also evident is a tree cutter, a man with an ax, whose action will fell the tree, in the course of which, Scripture forecasts, the birds and animals will be dispersed. But the tree's roots and stump fastened with iron and bronze will remain in the ground. In the dream-vision, an angel narrates the foregoing activities and others like them that will occur at the tree, though Daniel will interpret their significance for Nebuchodonosor.

The commentary stresses how these activities, both literally and figuratively, prefigure the crucifixion of Jesus. Literally, for instance, the metal at the roots and stump of the tree foreshadows that Jesus was bound to a column for scourging and that he was nailed to the cross; furthermore, the angel narrates that Nebuchodonosor will be dampened with dew, a prefiguration of Christ who will be bathed in his own blood. Figuratively, the animals in the dream-vision suggest the degradation that Scripture foretells concerning Nebuchodonosor, who for seven years will suffer penitentially for his misdeeds and sins, dwelling among, and eating like, the beasts, after which he will be restored to sovereignty in his realm. Selectively juxtaposing the plight of Nebuchodonosor with the Passion of Jesus, the commentary, among other things, asserts that the tormentors of Christ treat him as if they were predatory beasts and he were a beast victimized by them.

Figure 95. King Codrus gives his life for his subjects

From Valerius Maximus (*Valerii Maximi Factorum et Dictorum Memorabilium Libri Novem*, ed. C. Halm [Teubner Classics: Leipzig, 1865], book 5, chap. 6, ext 1) and also *Gesta Romanorum* (trans Rev. Charles Swan, rev. and corr. by Wynnard Hooper [London, 1905], chap. 41), this illustration and commentary present King Codrus of Athens. The king wished to lift the siege of the city, despite the fact that there were no prospective liberators. Consulting with Apollo, the king learned that his death at the hands of his enemies would save the city. Though the king went forth in order to die for his people, his enemies declined to slay him. Representing the role of King Codrus as a prefiguration of the voluntary self-sacrificial ministry of Jesus, the commentary by implication likens the enemy besieging Athens to the forces of evil that beleaguer humankind. In both instances, external intervention by King Codrus or by Jesus becomes necessary to relieve the subjects from the threat of their respective enemies. The typological resemblance continues between King Codrus and Jesus: the enemies of the king choose not to slay him, and the devil by implication strives to forestall the death of Jesus. The devil knows that the end of his power over humankind will occur when the redemptive ministry of Jesus is consummated. Despite the pagan era in which King Codrus lived and the secular nature of his power, the commentary dwells on the prefigurative significance of the monarch's loving self-sacrifice for his people and of his sovereignty over his realm. In doing so, the commentary characterizes King Codrus as anticipating both the redemptive ministry of Jesus on earth and his eternal kingdom in the hereafter. In doing so, the commentary operates on the assumption that earlier history acquires its greatest significance harmonized with the Christian view of salvation.

Figure 96. After Eleazer stabs the elephant, he is crushed by it

In 1 Machabees 6.42–46, Eleazar attacks an elephant bearing warriors. By stabbing the elephant under its belly, Eleazar, while slaying it, brings on his own death when the animal collapses on him. Before interpreting this biblical account of Eleazar's heroic deed, the commentary continues to analyze the story of King Codrus, indicating that the ruler of Athens disguises himself in servant's garb, departs the city in order to confront the enemy in his disguise, and suffers death because he goes unrecognized as king. When the enemy discover that they have slain the ruler of Athens, they call off the siege and return to their homeland. Similarly, Christ, who disguises his regal or deific nature behind the veil of his humanity, undergoes death and thereby liberates us from being captives of the devil. If the enemies of Jesus had seen him in the fullness of his glory, they would or could not have slain him.

Moving to the exploits of Eleazar, the commentary notes that by his own death he was able to slay the elephant, an instrument of death. Likewise, Jesus by dying frees humankind from death, which becomes the transition to the eternal afterlife. While the self-sacrifice of Jesus is one of voluntary humiliation, the triumph over death achieved thereby is couched in images, both visual and verbal, of a military feat, whether relieving people from siege or overcoming warriors atop an elephant or in the company of a menacing beast. However the victory is achieved, death's claim on humankind is of short duration, for in contrast to the eternity of the afterlife, any temporal period, even that awaiting the General Resurrection, is negligible. In the Providential plan, the sting of death, while aimed at a human being, ultimately and ironically becomes self-directed.

Chapter 25

Figure 97. Mary's sorrow for her Son

All four Gospels (Matthew 27.57–61, Mark 15.42–47, Luke 23.50–55, John 19.38–42) treat the deposition or removal of Christ from the cross, the basis of the illustration and commentary here. Joseph of Arimathea stands beneath Jesus, supporting the body as it is lowered from above by Nicodemus, who is on a ladder. Standing in the background are two Apostles: the bearded one presumably Peter, the younger one perhaps the beloved disciple cited in John's Gospel. In the foreground are two women: Mary Magdalen on her knees, and the Blessed Virgin at Christ's feet. The commentary focuses on the grief of Mary, who as *mater dolorosa*, or the sorrowful mother, undergoes empathetically the pain of her son, Jesus, during his Passion. As such, Mary fulfills the prophecy of Simeon at the Presentation of Jesus in the temple (Luke 2.35): that she will be pierced with a sword. Accordingly, Mary will suffer heartbreak at the suffering and death of her son because the greatest grief to befall a parent is to witness the death of one's child. Most of the commentary recounts the grief of Jacob over the presumed death of his favorite son, Joseph, as foreshadowing the Virgin Mary's sorrow over the crucifixion of Jesus. Drawing on Genesis 37, the commentary cites the coat that Jacob presented as a sign of special affection for his son. Divesting Joseph of the coat, his brothers tear it asunder, soil it with the blood of a goat, and send it to their father, who is distraught because he believes his favorite son has been killed by a wild beast. Jacob remains inconsolable. The brothers placed Joseph in a cistern, rather than slay him. But traders rescued him from his internment; and after their arrival in Egypt, they sold him to Potiphar, the chief steward of the Pharao (Genesis 37.36).

Figure 98. Jacob laments for his son Joseph

Jacob's lamentation over the death of Joseph, shown and glossed in this illustration and commentary, derives from Genesis 37.32–35. Continuing the typological relationship between Jacob's role as *pater dolorosus* (the sorrowful father) and Mary's as *mater dolorosa* (the sorrowful mother), the commentary stresses that both parents are inconsolable in the present life. Mary would have followed her son to limbo at his death, and Scripture recounts that Jacob wished to accompany his dead son to the nether world. Whereas Joseph's coat was rent asunder, the commentary likens that garment to the flesh of Jesus, which veiled his divinity and which was perforated at the Passion and crucifixion. If Joseph's attire was stained with the blood of a goat, the flesh of Jesus was soiled by his own bloodshed, the viciousness of his tormentors being likened to the frenzy of beasts. Jacob rends his own garments as a gesture of lamentation but also as an empathetic response to the sight of his son's own torn clothing, and grief over the death of Jesus overtakes Mary, thereby afflicting her inner self. Whereas the commentary does not mention the special significance of Joseph's coat, Scripture does. The coat was a gift from Jacob to his favorite son; and in part because they envied Joseph, the brothers disintegrate the garment. Analogously, the garb of flesh that Jesus wore over his divinity was a gift from the Father to humanity generally. In his incarnate nature rent by suffering, the Son became the sacrifice that provided the means for humankind's salvation. The commentary, with reference to Mary's sorrow over the loss of her only son, contends that it outweighs the grief of Jacob's presumed loss of one of many sons and exceeds that of Adam and Eve who mourned the death of Abel for more than 100 years.

Figure 99. The first parents mourn the death of Abel

Based on Genesis 4.1–14, which narrates the slaying of Abel, the illustration features Adam and Eve mourning their dead son. Both

parents are kneeling with their hands folded. Adam's digging implement is leaning against his right leg, a reminder that after the expulsion from Paradise, Adam must delve into the soil as part of the
labor required for survival. Recumbent on the earth, the slain Abel
is the first deceased human being. Adam's spade nearby will be
used, presumably, to dig the grave, a reminder that humankind
having been created from the earth will return to it. The attitude of
Adam and Eve, who are kneeling on the earth while viewing their
dead son, resembles that of Joseph and Mary in typical scenes of
the Nativity. But the joy at the birth of a son has given way to the
bitter sorrow of witnessing his death.

The ironic symmetry of joy and sorrow informs the reference to
the Canticle of Canticles (1.13) in the commentary. The beloved in
the Canticle likens her lover to a packet of myrrh at her bosom.
Used in making incense and perfume, the myrrh instead of produc-
ing a pleasurable sensation generates the very opposite, a bitterness, at the heart of the Virgin. This bitterness becomes the sorrow
of a broken heart. In line with this view, the myrrh for the Virgin is
a spice that she uses to anoint the body of her dead son. Another
Old Testament analogue of the Virgin's transformation of joy to sorrow is Noemi from the Book of Ruth (1.20), whose two sons died.
Fraught with sorrow, she renounces her name "Noemi," which
means amiable, pleasant, or beautiful. Instead of that name, she
adopts Mara, which means bitter, a view based on the perception
that God by the deaths of her sons has punished her for some evil.
In the case of the Virgin Mary, both she and her son are without
blame, but their bitterness results from the punishment that they
have accepted in place of culpable and fallen humankind.

Figure 100. Noemi bewails the death of her sons

From the Book of Ruth 1.20, which provides an analogue of the Virgin Mary's sorrow, this illustration features Noemi on her knees,
her hands clasped and close to her chest in a gesture of grief, signifying the sorrow in her heart. Lying on the ground are her two dead
sons. The commentary views this episode in the Book of Ruth as a

prefiguration of the Virgin Mary's two sons: Jesus, her natural son, and humankind, figuratively and collectively her adopted son. Whereas the former died in body, the latter did so in spirit. The death of her natural son is undertaken in order to revive the dead spirit of her adopted son — that is, to bring new spiritual life to fallen humankind. Framing this interactive relationship according to the practice of exchanging gifts, the commentary asserts that one tends to value more highly a gift received than one given. In line with this view, Mary's two sons, the one natural and the other adopted, are correlated as follows: the natural son, Jesus, is the gift given, whereas the adopted son, humankind, is the gift received. As such, Mary permits her natural son, Jesus, the gift that she gives, to die on behalf of her adopted son, humankind, the gift she has received. In other words, the crucifixion of Jesus counteracts the damnation of humankind, the one son being sacrificed for the other. At the same time, the commentary affirms that from the example of Mary, we may conclude that the Father's love for humankind is also boundless. The Father's gift of Jesus, the incarnate Son, to fallen humankind reflects the immensity of divine love, which redeems the adopted son, who is valued so dearly, from spiritual death.

Chapter 26

Figure 101. At Compline Jesus is buried

All four Gospels recount the burial of Jesus (Matthew 27.57–61, Mark 15.42–47, Luke 23.50–56, John 19.38–42). In the illustration, Joseph of Arimathea is at the head of Jesus, lowering him into the tomb, while Nicodemus holds the feet of Christ. The Virgin Mary leans over the recumbent body of Jesus, and behind her are two other women, perhaps Mary Magdalen, Mary the Mother of James, Salome, or Joanna, all of whom are cited in the Gospels. Between the two women appears the Beloved Disciple from John's Gospel. The commentary, which indicates that the burial takes place at Compline, the last of the seven canonical hours, perceives the entombment as the end of a funeral procession. As such, that procession becomes the counterpart of Christ's journey toward Golgotha along the *via dolorosa*. Scripturally and commemoratively, that earlier journey receives more attention, but the present illustration and commentary redress the imbalance, so to speak. If, therefore, the crucifixion is the climax of the *via dolorosa*, then the entombment consummates the journey from Golgotha to the site of Christ's burial. The journey along the *via dolorosa*, to be sure, focuses on Christ, but the procession from Golgotha to the tomb of Jesus dwells on the Virgin Mary as the grieving mother or *mater dolorosa*. Her passionate response to her dead son becomes a lamentation, and her affectionate interaction with his body becomes the maternal counterpart of Mary Magdalen's penitential and maudlin relationship with Jesus at the house of Simon, the Pharisee. Like Mary Magdalen, the Virgin Mary kisses the feet of Jesus. But unlike Mary Magdalen who weeps profusely because of her own sinfulness, the Virgin Mary grieves over the sins of humankind, on whose behalf her son suffered.

Figure 102. David weeps at the funeral for Abner

This derives from 2 Kings 3.31–38, in which David laments the death of Abner. David's own lamentation includes the rending of garments and a manifestation of grief so loud that the people joined in with their ruler. David, moreover, was inconsolable, abstaining from food during his lamentation. The commentary cites both the instinct of animals that are moved to sympathy when one of them is crying and the apparent practice of dolphins to mourn and bury their dead. The response that others make to the intense grief of a mourner becomes the context for understanding how and why the Virgin Mary effected a reaction among onlookers when she lamented Jesus' death. Adding to her grief is the realization that suffering and death were meted out wrongly to her son, who, while innocent, became thoroughly a victim of injustice. The commentary attributes to the Virgin Mary the comments that David utters to the people after Abner's death. What David said about Abner, the Virgin Mary may, or could, have said about Jesus: "Rend your garments, your interior spirit, and mourn with me!" By experiencing and manifesting grief from her innermost nature, the Virgin Mary has no recourse but to lament overtly, weep loudly, wring her hands, and strike her breast as a sign of a broken heart. Indeed, the rending of garments reflects externally the emotional disintegration of one's inner spirit. By its emphasis on the lamentation of the Virgin Mary, the commentary creates a strikingly different portrait of her from, say, Michelangelo's *Pietà*, where she appears resigned, stoical, even immobilized by her grief. The commentary tends to humanize, as well as idealize, the Virgin Mary in order to project her role as the natural mother of a dead son who was the victim of injustice.

Figure 103. Joseph is cast into the well

From Genesis 37.12–36, this illustration features the brothers of Joseph who place him in a dry cistern after taking his colorful coat. Rending his coat and soiling it with the blood of a goat, they present the garment to Jacob, who believes his son has been slain by a wild animal. Typologically, Joseph in the darkness and confinement of the cistern prefigures Jesus in his tomb. The torn and soiled coat anticipates the garb of flesh that Jesus wore over his divinity, garb rent asunder by the buffeting, scourging, and crucifixion and reddened by the issuance of blood from his wounds. The commentary distinguishes, however, the painless tearing of Joseph's coat from the painful wounds inflicted on Christ's flesh. One rendition of the story of Joseph in Genesis recounts that his brothers eventually withdrew him from the cistern, then sold him to traders enroute to Egypt, thereby foreshadowing how Judas betrayed Jesus for a price. The commentary, in locating the devil at the left side of the cross, may be alluding to one of the two criminals that in Luke 23.39 blasphemes Christ. Since the left side is typically the position of disfavor in parables centering upon damnation and salvation, the criminal crucified to the left of Jesus may signify the devil and may utter temptation comparable to what Christ encountered in the wilderness: that if he were the Son of God he would not suffer, for a respite from suffering would be provided by his own power or by the power of the Father who would intervene on his behalf. If, as well, the reference to the presence of the devil means that he is at the left brace or on the left of the transverse beam of the cross, the image is that of scales or balances, whereby the devil and those who yield to his wiles will be weighed at the Final Judgment, and by such means eternal justice will be determined.

Figure 104. A whale devours Jonas

The focus here is on the story of Jonas and the great fish from Jonas 1–2. Beset by a storm, mariners on a ship threw Jonas overboard to appease the Lord from whom the prophet was fleeing. The Lord sent a large fish to swallow Jonas, who remained in its belly for three days and nights, before he was spewed onto the shore. While in the belly of the fish, Jonas prayed to the Lord a psalm of thanksgiving, highlighting the dangers of being cast into the deep and enveloped by the abyss, but he was finally delivered from annihilation by the Lord. The commentary recounts Jonas's experience as a prefiguration of the three-day period when Christ was entombed. Much as Jonas was in the gullet of the fish, so too Jesus in his descent into, or harrowing of, hell, entered darkness and emerged from it, delivering from captivity the patriarchs, prophets, and kings of the Hebraic Dispensation. In effect, Jesus is a liberator, and the fish, its jaws suggesting the mouth of hell, is a place of imprisonment.

At the same time, the commentary implies a sacramental counterpart for Christians who, like Jonas, undergo the threat of inundating waters. Romans 6.3 and Colossians 2.12 indicate that at baptism one is buried with Christ, a statement suggesting that immersion in water is the mimetic and symbolic counterpart of being threatened by the deep or the abyss. Emergence from the water signifies deliverance from that threat. This cycle of immersion and emergence is enacted variously in Scripture, ranging from the Deluge in Genesis and the issuance of Noe and his family from the ark to the deliverance of the Chosen People, who while threatened by the walls of water in the Red Sea emerge unharmed. Jonah's experience and every baptized Christian's mimetic and sacramental enactment of immersion and emergence suggest burial with Christ but eventual participation in his Resurrection.

Chapter 27

Figure 105. The holy patriarchs are freed from the lower world

From Ephesians 4.9 and 1 Peter 3.19, this illustration and commentary deal with Christ's descent into, or harrowing of, hell. The illustration depicts hell as a fortress, at whose ramparts and apertures both demons and flames appear. The access to the fortress is through the mouth or jaws of a monster, presumably Leviathan, whose teeth are evident and from whom flames also emerge. Its jaws unhinged, Leviathan yields its captives to Jesus, the deliverer, who with his right hand escorts the first of the fathers out of captivity. Presumably this is Adam, behind whom stands Eve, followed, in turn, by a multitude of others. In his left hand, Jesus holds aloft a triumphal cross, which is very different from the cross of humiliation and suffering that he carried along the *via dolorosa* and on which he was crucified. The triumphal cross resembles a lance, one of the *arma Christi* or weapons of Christ that he deploys against the devil. It also suggests a military insignia or ensign: a pennon emblazoned with a cross, which is first held by Jesus but thereafter adopted by every Christian in his or her struggle against the devil. The commentary stresses that Christ's visit to the underworld occurred on Good Friday, a gesture of consolation to the imprisoned souls and a sign of their imminent deliverance. By such conduct, Jesus is the prototype of the compassionate liberator who provides immediate hope by his visit and ongoing presence. He succors the captives and alleviates their anguish by promising an end to their captivity, whose indefinite term had only intensified their suffering. Having suffered so extremely himself, he now affords sympathy and relief to others whose faith and hope are tested by adversity.

Figure 106. Israel's liberation from the Pharao

Israel's liberation from Egypt is recounted in Exodus 14. Pictured here are Moses, with rod uplifted, and the Israelites — men, women, and children — who have prepared for travel and follow behind him. Beginning with the episode at the burning bush, the commentary dwells on the Lord who reveals himself to Moses and who summons that shepherd to be his prophet and minister. Using the Israelites' liberation as a typological prefiguration of humankind's deliverance from the devil's tyranny, the commentary cites numerous psalmic pleas to the Lord for assistance; these echo the cries of the Israelites and anticipate the petitions of the faithful since the inception of Christianity. Informing all such pleas is humankind's dependence on the Lord. With the Incarnation of the Son and his ministry of redemption, both the faithful of the Old Law and the followers of Christ under the New Law are liberated. Because of the importance of the Incarnation, the commentary, echoing traditional exegesis, likens the phenomenon of the burning bush, aptly termed a sign and wonder, to the mysterious impregnation of the Virgin Mary. If the bush remains intact despite the flames, then Mary though impregnated continues to be virginal. Much as the Lord smites the pharao in order to deliver the Israelites from bondage, so too Christ assaults the devil and his demons at their fortress during the harrowing of hell. Finally, Canaan, described as a land of milk and honey, anticipates the festive banquet in the eternal afterlife. While the commentary does not explicitly state the typological similarity, Canaan as a land of natural bounty foreshadows the Eucharistic repast, which is fulfilled by the nuptial feast of the lamb in the hereafter.

Figure 107. The liberation of Abraham from Ur of the Chaldees

From Genesis 11–15 and also Peter Comestor's *Historia Scholastica* (*PL*, CXCVIII, 1091), the illustration and commentary center on the migration of Abraham from Ur of the Chaldeans, which typifies the nomadic life of God's Chosen People until they settle eventually in Canaan. Augmenting the scriptural account is the legendary narrative of Abraham's refusal to acknowledge the god of the Chaldeans, who worshiped fire. After Abraham is cast into fire by the Chaldeans, the Lord rescues him. In the illustration, the Lord appears in the clouds, and with his arms stretched downward, he grasps the hands of Abraham to elevate him from the flames. Willing to be a sacrifice, Abraham — whose fidelity to the Lord has been tested to the limit — achieves a purified state as the minister of the Lord. With Abraham's self-sacrifice as a prototype, the commentary cites the slaughtered lambs whose blood the Chosen People used to mark their doorposts and lintels so that the Lord would not strike down their firstborn. Similarly, the Lord in order to liberate humankind sacrifices himself through the Incarnate Son in what is tantamount to an immolation or a holocaust. In doing so, he voluntarily accepts the pain and suffering that are due to humankind. This tendency of the Lord to relieve others of pain and suffering is reenacted in the descent into hell, when Jesus by announcing the impending liberation of the holy fathers terminates their anguish. Even before Jesus escorts the holy fathers to their eternal banquet, the commentary likens his appearance to them as a means of feeding and succoring: his humanity is like milk; his divinity as they contemplate it is like honey.

Figure 108. The liberation of Lot from Sodom

Deriving from Genesis 19.12–29, this depicts Lot's liberation from Sodom. Two angels sent by the Lord to destroy the cities of the Plain, Sodom and Gomorrah, warned Lot to flee to safety with his family; for he was deemed to be innocent, rather than wicked like all the other inhabitants. Taking his wife and two daughters, Lot escaped as sulphurous fire rained down on the cites. His wife, however, violated the instruction of the divine messengers, who cautioned Lot's family not to pause or to look back as they fled to safety. She was turned into a pillar of salt. Using the escape of Lot, his sorrow in abandoning his home, and the hardship of his travel, the commentary dwells on the adversities that the Lord visits mercifully on his people. Intended to test his people, to enrich their patience, to induce a penitential state, and to purify them of their love of ease and prosperity, these adversities induce a benign suffering whose long-term effect will be to rescue the Lord's people from eternal damnation. Accordingly, Lot and his family as they ascend from the cites of the Plain typify the arduous journey of the faithful whose gradual rise through a hierarchy of virtues and meritorious deeds enables them never to look back on the sinfulness they have rejected. Likewise suggested is the Lord's separation of the damned, who are punished in the destruction of Sodom and Gomorra, and the redeemed, like Lot, who escape the torment. In line with this outlook, Lot's escape anticipates the liberation of the holy fathers from hell. The disobedience of Lot's wife and her conversion to stony salt, which is licked by beasts, designate both the hardened heart of the obdurate sinner and the degradation of the sinner.

Chapter 28

Figure 109. The Resurrection of our Lord Jesus Christ

The glorification and exaltation of Jesus at the Resurrection, in line with the scriptural account in Mark 28, feature an angel who shone like lightning and overwhelmed the guards at the tomb of Jesus. In the illustration, the guards are either sleeping, because the Resurrection occurred at or shortly before dawn, or suffering from temporary blindness and shock because of their encounter with the bright angel. Because the resurrected Christ is the focus of the illustration, the risen Lord, instead of the angel as his harbinger, appears before dawn while the guards are asleep. Or in the illustration Christ's resplendent glorification and exaltation replace and supersede the role of the angel in Scripture, overwhelming the guards. Christ assumes the attitude of a triumphant warrior, *Christus victor*; and with his left hand, he holds the triumphal cross, while his right hand is elevated victoriously. The commentary stresses that

Christ was placed in a traditional Jewish sepulchre, carved out of rock and consisting of two rooms. While the usual security for such a sepulchre included a heavy stone at the door and a seal, the presence of guards afforded added protection that the body of Christ would not be stolen, an action that the chief priests and Pharisees feared. They recalled the prophecy of Jesus that he would rise from the dead after three days (John 2.18). If his body were removed by his disciples, they could contend that he was risen. But at the Resurrection and afterwards in post-Resurrectional appearances, Christ miraculously travels through closed and locked doors, unimpeded by physical barriers. Perhaps he achieves an apparitional or rarefied state as a sign of his imminent return heavenward.

Figure 110. Samson carries off the gates of Gaza

From Jonas 2.11, this illustration and commentary, which reflect Judges 16.1–3, present Samson, who has unhinged the gates to the Philistine city of Gaza, as prefiguring Christ during the three-day period after his death. Alerted that Samson would be in Gaza, the Philistines encircled him at night and guarded the gate to the city, where in the morning they planned to assault him. At midnight, however, Samson removed the doors of the gates, along with the posts, hoisted them onto his shoulders, and carried them to a hilltop opposite Hebron. While the commentary does not dwell on typological resemblances to the passion of Christ, one may argue that the plan to apprehend Jesus at Gethsemane reenacts the Philistine plot to engage Samson in Gaza. Furthermore, by transporting the gates and their posts on his shoulders and carrying them to a hilltop, Samson anticipates the carrying of the cross to Golgotha. But the commentary focuses more on the typological role of Samson foreshadowing both the harrowing of hell and the Resurrection of Jesus. Much as Samson spends the night surrounded by his enemies, so too Jesus remains in limbo until the darkness preceding Easter Sunday. And if Samson victoriously emerges, after having unhinged the restraints intended to prevent his exit from Gaza, then Jesus opens the jaws or gates of limbo to lead forth the holy fathers. At his Resurrection Jesus again emerges victoriously from the restraints at the sepulcher: the heavy stone at the doorway and the seal. He triumphs over the guards whose duty it was to prevent his body from being removed from its resting place. The commentary, in accordance with Matthew 27.52–53, indicates that the bodies of the holy fathers rose with Jesus because their souls having been liberated from limbo were reunited with their bodies in the graves.

Figure 111. The emergence of Jonas

The emergence of Jonas from the whale is based on Jonas 2.11. Jonas prefigures both the issuance of the souls of the holy fathers from limbo and the egress of their bodies from graves on earth. After their souls had been liberated from limbo, the bodies of the holy fathers emerged from graves on earth as a consequence of the Resurrection of Jesus. Without having to undergo death again, the holy fathers later ascended heavenward with Jesus. The commentary relates Jonas's three-day captivity in the whale and eventual emergence to the Resurrection of Christ. The commentary also correlates the turbulent sea into which Jonas was tossed to the adversities and instability of the human condition, those challenges and dangers that threaten the loss of eternal life. Much as the sea became calm after Jonas was submerged in it, so also Christ's immersion in the human condition, death, and Resurrection assuage our fears regarding the loss of eternal life. His sacrifice, in short, restores the hope of our salvation. As verbal shorthand for this multifarious role of Jesus, the commentary describes him as the "firstborn of the dead," a phrase appropriated from Colossians 1.18 and appearing also in 1 Corinthians 15–20 with some variation, where Christ is described as the "first fruits of those who have fallen asleep." But 1 Corinthians broadens the significance of the account of Jonas and the whale and Christ's death and Resurrection to include the faithful at large. Paul argues in 1 Corinthians 15.21–29 that if the dead are not to be raised at the Second Coming, what is the purpose of Baptism, a sacramental celebration that inducts us into the memory of the dead while also affirming our faith in, and hope for, their and our eventual resurrection. Not to be overlooked is the typological similarity of the waters that engulfed Jonas and from which he emerged and the use of water in the baptismal celebration.

Figure 112. The rejected block is made the cornerstone

From Psalm 117.22, which is echoed in Matthew 21.42 and 1 Peter 2.4–7, this illustration and commentary focus on the construction of the temple and its completion when the builders select a block that they previously rejected for any use at all. In this instance, the block becomes the cornerstone or keystone that connects the two walls. The thrust of the saying — "That stone that the builders rejected has become the cornerstone" (Psalms 117.22) — dramatizes that the Lord's ways are mysterious and that Providential intent or design as it unfolds is not fully understandable to humankind. The commentary focuses on Christ as the cornerstone or keystone, who had been rejected at his passion but who becomes essential by his Resurrection to the connection of the two walls of the temple. These two walls signify the Jews and the Gentiles who are joined together through Christ into one church. The illustration and the commentary, while promoting the idea of an ecclesiastical building, also verge on the concept, recurrent in Paul's epistles, of the church as the mystical body with Christ as its head, its principal source of integration of the disparate parts or limbs, and its vitalizing agent. Likewise, the illustration and commentary glance toward the concept of sacramental celebration in an ecclesiastical community. By mentioning the body and blood of Jesus, the commentary presents the Eucharistic celebration as a crucial means of uniting a community of the faithful in the very presence of Jesus. Such a sacramental celebration also commemorates the relationship of Jesus and his disciples, who in a certain sense constituted the first Christian community or church.

Chapter 29

Figure 113. The Last Judgment

Figure 113 deals with Doomsday and the Last Judgment as re-counted in Matthew 24.29–31, Mark 13.24–27, and Revelation 4.2–3 and 20.11–13. At the very top of the illustration are the flared ends of horns through which angels are sounding the call for Doomsday, at which the graves, illustrated at the bottom, are open-ing. Enthroned on the arch or vault of the firmament, Jesus wears a regal garment, and his feet rest on a sphere that signifies the earth. This image derives from several passages in Scripture, most notably Isaiah 66.1, Matthew 5.35 and Acts of the Apostles 7.49, all of which state that the heavens are the throne of the Lord and the earth his footstool. The garment of Jesus is parted to reveal his wounds, and his arms are extended in the attitude of crucifixion because his judgment of the multitudes at Doomsday will center on their observance or rejection of the doctrine of the cross, which he affirms in the Gospels. In Matthew 16.24–28, for instance, Jesus asserts that a man or woman who follows him will deny oneself, take up one's cross, and walk in his footsteps. Also evident along-side the head of Jesus are a sword to his left and a sprig of flowers, probably lilies, to his right. Numerous parables, to be sure, antici-pate the separation of the saved from the damned, associating the former with the right side and the latter with the left side. Appro-priately, therefore, the sword is a punitive instrument to be applied to the damned, whereas the lilies, which typically represent the Annunciation and the purity of the Virgin Mary, signify the holiness and sanctification that will characterize the souls to be saved by the mercy and grace from the Lord. Below and kneeling are inter-cessors on behalf of humankind, probably the Virgin Mary and St. Joseph. Their presence with Jesus reunites the holy family on earth.

Figure 114. The nobleman returns from afar and makes an accounting

From Matthew 25.14–30 and Luke 19.11–27, this emphasizes the strictness of the Last Judgment. In the illustration, the master has returned to his household, after having journeyed to a faraway land to acquire another kingdom. Before he departs, he lends his servants money to invest, and at his return he summons them to an accounting. He then rewards his servants after having judged whether they acquired greater or lesser profits from their use of the money. Toward the servant who made no profit, the master is harsh, ordering him to be cast into the darkness outside where there are weeping and the grinding of teeth. The illustration shows that servant being cast into a pit, which signifies the infernal region, whose tormented inhabitants weep and grind their teeth because of the pain that afflicts them.

The commentary implies resemblance between Jesus at the Second Coming and the master who insists on strict accounting from his servants. Both will be impelled by vengeance. If the master does not enjoy a profitable return from his loan to the one servant, Jesus, despite his suffering and crucifixion on behalf of humanity, will judge some of the people to have performed few if any good works. In other words, his consummate good work is met with ingratitude by the very people for whom it was intended as an act of redemption. The commentary also stresses the wholesale rejection at the Last Judgment of the sinner who has no advocates. Even Nature and its four elements that sustained the sinner take up the case against him. His guardian angel will affirm sinfulness on the part of the very person to whom he futilely offered protection, and the Virgin Mary, though known as the Mother of Mercy and helpful to sinners in the present life, will not plead the case of the damned at the Last Judgment.

Figure 115. The kingdom of Heaven is like the ten virgins

The parable of the wise and foolish virgins, from Matthew 25.1–12, is the topic here. The illustration depicts the ten women, five on either side of the bridegroom for whom they had been waiting. In front of an open door, he stands in judgment over them, rejecting the five virgins to his left, and welcoming the five to his right. The rejected virgins, some of whom look forlornly toward the bridegroom above, descend the steps and enter the outstretched jaws of hell, in which flames are evident. In their hands, they carry unlit lamps. The virgins whom the bridegroom welcomes ascend the steps toward his outstretched arms, and each of them has a lamp that is lit, from which a tongue of fire issues forth to provide light. All ten virgins together had been awaiting the arrival of the bridegroom, who delayed his coming. Whereas the wise virgins brought a supply of oil for their lamps, the foolish virgins did not. When all ten had fallen asleep, the bridegroom arrived. At about midnight, someone shouted that the bridegroom was present, and all the virgins awakened. When the foolish virgins sought to borrow oil to resupply their lamps, the wise virgins declined and followed the bridegroom to the wedding, at which the door was barred. When the foolish virgins, having gone off to purchase more oil, returned, they were denied access to the wedding. The purpose of the parable is to highlight the uncertainty of the moment of the Second Coming. A keen expectation and a state of readiness characterize the souls eager to meet, greet, and be wedded to the bridegroom, whereas a lack of preparedness distinguishes those souls that will be damned.

Figure 116. The hand of God writes on the wall

This is based on Daniel 5, centering upon an Old Testament prefiguration of the Last Judgment. Pictured are King Belshazzar to the left and Daniel to the right. Under the influence of wine, the king who had given a banquet for 1,000 of his lords ordered for their use the golden and silver vessels that his father, King Nebuchodonosor, had taken from the temple of the Lord in Jerusalem. While the lords were drinking wine from the vessels, a human hand appeared and inscribed a message on the wall of the king's palace. Troubled by this intervention, the king summoned all of the wise men of Babylon to decipher the message. Not one of them was successful, so that the queen recommended Daniel, who interpreted the writing. Like King Nebuchodonosor, his father, King Belshazzar at the height of his power and glory became insolent and arrogant. King Nebuchodonosor was humbled by the Lord, stripped of his regal accouterments and trappings, and lived with the animals. Daniel faults King Belshazzar who knew of the experiences of his father but did not humble his own heart. Therefore, the message of three words in Aramaic and Daniel's interpretation thereof are: (1) "Mane," that God has numbered Belshazzar's kingdom and ended it, (2) "Thechel," that Belshazzar has been weighed on the scales and found lacking, (3) "Phares," that Belshazzar's kingdom has been divided and given to others. Using Daniel's interpretation of the threefold judgment of Belshazzar — by number, weight, and division — the commentary explains how the Last Judgment will be conducted under the omniscience of the Lord.

SELECTED BIBLIOGRAPHY

In addition to references fully cited in our interpretations of the woodcuts and commentaries, we provide the following entries with additional information concerning *The Mirror of Salvation* and also *The Bible of the Poor*:

Barr, James. *Old and New in Interpretation: A Study of Two Testaments* (London: SCM Press, 1966).

Bliss, Douglas P. *A History of Wood-Engraving* (London: Dent, 1928).

Didron, Adolphe Napoléon. *Christian Iconography*, 2 vols., trans. E. J. Millington (New York: Frederick Ungar Publishing Co., 1965).

Henry, Avril. *Biblia Pauperum: A Facsimile and Edition* (Ithaca, NY: Cornell University Press, 1987).

Henry, Avril. *The Mirour of Mans Saluacion, A Middle English translation of the Speculum Humanae Salvationis* (Philadelphia: University of Pennsylvania Press, 1987).

Huth, A. H. *The Miroure of Man's Saluacionne. A fifteenth-century translation into English of the Speculum Humanae Salvationis and Now for the First Time Printed from a Manuscript in the Possession of Alfred Henry Huth* (London: Roxburghe Club 118, 1888).

Mâle, Emile. *The Gothic Image: Religious Art in France of the Thirteenth Century*, trans. Dora Nussey (New York: Harper Torchbooks, 1958).

Migne, J.-P. *Patrologiae Cursus Completus . . . Series Latinae*. 221 volumes, Supplement 3 volumes. Paris, 1878–1890 and 1958–1963. Abbreviated as *PL*.

Labriola, Albert C., and John W. Smeltz. *The Bible of the Poor [Biblia Pauperum]: A Facsimile and Edition of the British Library Blockbook C.9 D.2* (Pittsburgh: Duquesne University Press, 1990).

Réau, Louis. *Iconographie d l'art Chrétien*, 6 vols. (Paris: Presses Universitaires de France, 1955–1959).

Scheller, Robert W. *A Survey of Medieval Model Books*, trans. D. A. S. Reid (Haarlem: Bohn, 1963).

Schiller, Gertrud. *Iconography of Christian Art*, 2 vols., trans. Janet Seligman (Greenwich, CT: New York Graphic Society LTD, 1971).

Smalley, Beryl. *The Study of the Bible in the Middle Ages*, 2nd ed. (Oxford: Oxford University Press, 1952).

INDEX

Aaron, 33, 36, 41, 108, 115, 139
Abel, 53, 66, 85, 146, 169–70
Abiron, 50
Abisai, 34, 59
Abner, 68, 172–73
Abraham, 31, 49, 60–61, 71, 92, 104–05, 138–39, 158–60, 176–77
Achab, 45
Achior, 45, 56–57, 151–52
Acts of the Apostles, 112, 182
Ada, 57
Adam, 18, 20–21, 21, 42, 60, 67, 80–81, 83–85, 98–99, 126, 169–70, 175
Amalecities, 104
Amasa, 52, 144–45
Ammonites, 59, 96–97, 151
Amon, 38, 119
Amos, 61
Amram, 38
angels, 20, 22-26, 30, 31–33, 38, 42–43, 59, 61, 64–65, 72, 79–80, 84, 87, 90, 99–103, 135, 139, 177
angus Dei, 104, 136
Anna, 23, 26, 37, 87, 91, 95–96, 114, 116–17
Annas, 54, 150
Annunciation, 4, 30, 87, 89, 91, 102–03, 107, 182
Antioclus, 51
antitypes, 2, 4
Apocalypse, 70
Apocrypha, 4, 6–7, 87, 155
The Apocrypha and Pseudiepigraphia of the Old Testament in English, (Charles, ed.), 130, 155, 162
Apollo, 65
Apostles, 25, 35, 52–53, 94, 112, 122–25, 144–45
Ark of Noe. *See* Noah's ark

Ark of the Covenant, 36, 114, 124–25
Ark of the Testament. *See also* ark of the Covenant, 36–37, 41
arma Christi, 175
Ascension, 111
Asia Minor, 109, 111
Asmodeus, 100
Assumption, 115
Assyrians, 130
Astyages, King, 22–23, 88, 92
Athens, 65
Augustine, Saint, 131
Augustus, 33

Babylon, 22–23, 34, 42–43, 46, 60, 88, 118, 130
Balaam, 23, 30, 90
Balac, 90
Balthassar, King, 75
Balthazar, 34
Banaias, 34
baptism, 40–43, 80, 121–24, 129, 157, 174
Barabbas, 60, 158
Baris tower, 29, 100–01
Bel, 43, 126–28
Belshazzar, King, 184–85
Bethlehem, 34, 39, 110
The Bible of the Poor, See also Biblia Pauperum, 3, 4, 7
Biblia Pauperum Bible of the Poor. See also The Bible of the Poor, 3
biblical typology, 2–3
blockbook, vii, 3–6
burning bush, 30, 31, 70, 103–04, 140, 176

Caesar Augustus, 33, 56, 109–10
Cain, 53, 66, 85, 146

189